POWERS OF ATTORNEY

I would like to thank my Secretary, Carolyn Armstrong, for her unending patience and tolerance during the preparation of this and other books.

POWERS OF ATTORNEY

PETER WADE

www.emeraldpublishing.co.uk

Emerald Guides

© Copyright Peter Wade 2015

ISBN: 9781847165862

Powers of Attorney

Contents

1

Lasting Powers of Attorney

Lasting Power of Attorney is a legal document which gives authority to another person to make decisions on your behalf. This is obviously someone you can trust to make decisions on your behalf. The Attorney you choose will be able to make decisions for you when you become lacking in mental capacity or simply no longer wish to do so

There are two types of Lasting Power of Attorney. There is:

- Property and Financial Lasting Power of Attorney, which allows your attorney to deal with your property and finances.

- Health and Welfare which allows your attorney to make care decisions on your behalf when you lack mental capacity to do so.

A Lasting Power of Attorney cannot be used until it is registered with the Office of the Public Guardian.

By having a Lasting Power of Attorney you are ensuring a safe way of having decisions made for you. The following reasons for this are:

- It has to be registered with the Office of the Public Guardian before it can be used

- You can choose someone to provide a 'certificate', which means they confirm that you understand the significance and purpose of what you're agreeing to. This is normally a solicitor or legal expert

- You can choose who gets told about your Lasting Power of Attorney when it is registered (so they have an opportunity to raise concerns). This may be a relative or someone close to you

- Your signature and the signatures of your chosen attorneys must be witnessed

- Your attorney(s) must follow the Code of Practice of the Mental Capacity Act 2005 and act in your best interests

- The Office of the Public Guardian provides helpful support and advice

2

The Mental Capacity Act 2005

The Attorney's must follow the code of the Mental Capacity Act 2005. Copies of this can be obtained from direct.gov.uk/mental capacity.

The main principles of the Act are:

- They must assume that you can make your own decisions

- They must help you to make as many decisions as you can

Your Attorney's must make decisions and act in your best interests when you are unable to make the decisions yourself.

What is Mental Capacity?

In everyday life we make decisions about various matters in our lives. We call this ability to make these decision 'Mental Capacity'

Some people may experience some difficulty in making decisions and this may be due to various reasons such as, a mental health problem, a learning disability or have had a stroke or brain injury.

The Mental Capacity Act of 2005 has more guidance on how to assess someone's ability to make decisions

This act covers decisions in areas such as property and financial affairs and health and welfare etc. It also covers everyday decisions such as personal care.

The Act also sets out five principles that are the basis of the legal requirement of the Act.

Unless it can be proved otherwise, every adult has the right to make their own decisions. All available help must be given before they are deemed not to be able to make their own decisions.

Any decision made for a person who is unable to so for themselves must be done in their best interests. Any decisions made for someone else should not restrict their basic rights and freedoms.

The Court of Protection has the power to make decisions about whether someone lacks mental capacity. It can also appoint deputies to act and make decisions on behalf of someone who is unable to do so on their own.

3

Enduring Powers of Attorney (EPA's)

No more Enduring Powers of Attorney may be created after the 1st October 2008, but there are Enduring Powers of Attorney which are in existence and they are perfectly legally valid.

It is a legal document by which the Donor give the legal right to one or more Attorney's to manage the Donor's property and financial affairs.

The document allows the Attorney's to do anything that the Donor would have been able to do for themselves.

General Powers of Attorney

A General Power of Attorney can still be created but this ends when the Donor lacks mental capacity, but an Enduring Power of Attorney continues even once this capacity no longer exists.

Under an enduring Power of Attorney, once the Donor becomes mentally incapable the Attorney will need to apply to Register the Enduring Power of Attorney with the OPG.

Enduring Powers of Attorney were created under the Enduring

Powers of Attorney Act 1985 which has been repealed by the Mental Capacity Act of 2005. The capacity to create an EPA was assumed to exist unless it was proven to the contrary.

If a person has mental capacity then Enduring Power of Attorney can be used like an Ordinary Power of Attorney. Once the mental capacity has lost this has to be registered.

Under an Enduring Power of Attorney, Attorney's may be appointed jointly or jointly and severally. Whereas with a single Attorney, that Attorney should sign on each occasion where two or more Attorneys are appointed they can be joint or joint and several. Jointly means both Attorney's need to sign on every occasion. Joint and Several means that either of the Attorneys could both sign but are not required to sign on each occasion. Both are not required to sign on each occasion.

Registration of an EPA

When an Attorney has reason to believe that the Donor has become mentally incapable he must apply to register the EPA.

Registration is made by completing the prescribed forms and giving notice to certain individuals who are entitled to receive notice of the intended registration.

Various parties are entitled to receive notice of intention to register and notice should be sent to:

- The Donor
- The Attorney's
- Close relatives of the Donor

There is a list of relatives to whom the notice should be given. Once up to three close relatives have been notified the provisions have been complied with.

****

4

The Difference Between Enduring Powers Of Attorney and Lasting Powers of Attorney

There cannot now be created an Enduring Power of Attorney, since the 30th September 2007.

With a Lasting Power of Attorney, it must contain names or persons who the donor wishes to be notified of any application and also must contain the Certificate that the donor understands the purpose of the instrument.

Decisions made under an LPA/EPA

Under an EPA the attorneys can do anything with the Donor's property and financial affairs, but cannot make decisions about the Donor's personal welfare.

Under an LPA the Attorney's can make decisions about property and financial affairs and personal welfare, including refusing consent to treatment.

The latter applies only if the Donor lacks, or that the Attorney reasonably believes that the Donor lacks mental capacity.

5

Who Can Create a Lasting Power of Attorney?

Anyone can create a Lasting Power of Attorney and it can also be described as the Capacity, that is those who are able make a Lasting Power of Attorney.

The Donor (the person making the LPA) has to be at least 18 years of age and has to have the mental capacity to execute under the Mental Health Act 2005.

The definition of lack of capacity is if a person lacks capacity in relation to a matter if at the material time he is unable to make a decision for himself in relation to the matter because of an impairment or of a disturbance in the functioning of the mind or brain. This may be either a temporary or permanent disturbance.

There is a presumption that a person can be assumed to have mental capacity unless it is established that he lacks capacity.

All persons over the age of 18 years of age are presumed to be capable of making their own decisions. The standard of proof is on a balance of probabilities. The Lasting Power of Attorney includes a certificate by a person of a prescribed description that at the time the

Donor executes the instrument that;

- The Donor understood the purpose of the instrument and the scope of the authority conferred under it.

- No fraud or undue pressure is used to induce the Donor to create an LPA

- There is nothing else which would prevent an LPA from being created from the instrument.

The current Fees for Registering a Lasting Power of Attorney are £130.00.

The Lasting Power of Attorney can be cancelled at any time as long as the person giving it has mental capacity to cancel

What happens if there is no LPA?

If there is no LPA then an application will need to be made to the Court of Protection at considerably more cost and with no guarantee that the right person will be appointed as the Deputy as it is named.

6

Creating a Lasting Power of Attorney

The forms can be found on the Ministry of Justice website. These forms are also contained in the appendix to this book.

The Registration must be done correctly and if there is a defect in the form may result in the refusal of the registration.

Once the LPA has been signed errors cannot be simply corrected although the OPG may allow certain amendments.

Executing the LPA – it must be signed by the Donor, the Certificate provider and the Attorneys in the correct order.

Execution by the Donor or the Attorneys must take place in the presence of a witness.

Restrictions on who can act as a witness are:

- The Donor and the Attorney must not witness each other's signature.

It is also suggested that neither the Donor's spouse or civil partner witness the LPA.

7

When Can it be Used – Or When Does the Instrument Come into Effect?

An EPA or an LPA only comes into effect when the Donor has become mentally incapable and will remain in operation provided it is registered.

Under an LPA it only becomes operable once it is registered with the Office of the Public Guardian.

This can take a number of weeks for registration to complete and the LPA cannot be used until this has been completed

The Office of the Public Guardian will give notice of the registration application to you or the Attorney(s). They will allow a period of five weeks waiting period in which you or the Attorney's may object to the registration. If the Donor objects to the registration then it can only go ahead if the Court is satisfied that the donor lacks the capacity to object.

8

Who Can be an Attorney?

Anyone over the age of 18 having mental capacity can be an Attorney, but there are factual grounds which may stop this such as:

- The Attorney is bankrupt.

- That the Attorney lacks capacity

- The Attorney has signed a Disclaimer

It is important to realise that anyone you appoint as your Attorney under a Lasting Power of Attorney will need, at some point to make important decisions for you.

You may decide to appoint a solicitor or other legal expert as an Attorney, however you must bear in mind that professional people may charge for their services. If however you choose a friend or relative as an Attorney they may be able to claim out of pocket expenses. However they cannot charge for their time unless the Donor has already agreed this on the LPA form. A donor can choose to have more than one Attorney which means that they can act together or independently and you will need to decide this. The obvious advantage of this is that it is harder for one Attorney to commit fraud and or act against the interests of the Donor.

If something happens to one of the Attorneys, and they are unable to act, there will be another one or two who can act as well. You may however have a good reason not to do this.

You can choose up to five people who can be named but one is sufficient. These can include family members but not your lawyers or certificate providers.

9

Duties of an Attorney Under a Lasting Power of Attorney

The Attorney's need to apply to the Court of Protection for Registration if they have reason to believe that the Donor has become mentally incapable.

Under a Lasting Power of Attorney they must act in accordance with the Mental Capacity Act 2005 and in the Donor's best interest and with regard to the Code of Practice.

The Attorney has the duty to act in the scope of the Lasting Power of Attorney subject to the MCA 2005 particularly the principles and best interests.

In addition they have a duty of care. This is one of care to:

- Carry out the Donor's instructions
- Not to take advantage of the position of the Attorney
- Not to delegate unless authorised to do so
- Of good faith
- Confidentiality to comply with directions of the Court of Protection

- Not to disclaim without notifying the Donor or the other Attorneys and the Public Guardian and complying with relevant guidance.

In relation to property and financial affairs there is an additional duty to keep account and keep the Donor's money and property separate from their own.

If the Attorneys are professional Attorneys they should demonstrate a higher degree of care and skill and they must also follow their professional rules and standards.

10

Gifts

In connection with a property and financial affairs Lasting Power of Attorney, the Attorney's have limited authority to make gifts of a donor's money or property if the recipient of the gift is related to or connected with the Donor or a charity to which the Donor actually made gifts or might be expected to make gifts if they had capacity.

A gift to a charity may be made at any time of the year, but a Gift to an individual might be of a seasonal nature, i.e. birth, marriage anniversary.

The value of the gift must not be unreasonable having regard to the circumstances. Gifts are not permitted to be made by the Attorney of your assets unless:

a) The recipient of the gift is an individual who is related to or connected with you or a charity to which you actually made gifts or might be expected to make gifts.
b) The timing of the gift must be of a seasonable nature or made on the occasion of a birth or marriage/civil partnership or on the anniversary of a birth or marriage/civil partnership.

c) The value of the gift must not be unreasonable having regard to all the circumstances and in particular the size of your estate.

If you wish you can totally restrict or exclude the ability to make any gifts or limit these.

The Court of Protection can authorise the Attorney to act so as to benefit themselves or otherwise provided there are no restrictions in the LPA itself and the Court is satisfied that this would be in your best interests.

11

When Should the LPA Be Registered?

Lasting Power of Attorney Registration
When should my LPA be registered?
Your LPA can be registered at any time after it has been completed and properly signed. The advantage to having it registered right away is that the LPA can be used by the Attorney whenever it is needed. If a long time passes before your LPA is registered, your circumstances may have changed and your LPA may no longer reflect your needs. If this is the case, you will not be able to modify your signed and completed LPA. You will have to create a new LPA.

Who can register my LPA?
Either the donor or the attorney may apply to register the LPA as long as the proper forms have been completed and all people who are to be notified have been notified.

Who must be notified of the application to register the LPA?
All named persons identified on pages 11 and 12 of the LPA must be notified. If you are an attorney making the application, you are not required to notify the Donor (although its strongly recommended that you discuss your intention to register with the donor). The Office of the Public Guardian will formally notify the Donor.

If I am an attorney acting together with another attorney, can I make an application on my own?
No, all attorneys appointed together must make an application together.

If I am an attorney acting together and independently with another attorney, can I make an application on my own?
You may make an application on your own, however it is a good idea to discuss your intention to apply for registration with all other attorneys. If the other attorneys know and approve of the registration, then your registration is less likely to encounter any challenges.

What forms should I use to register an LPA?
You require the form LPA001(see appendix): Notice of intention to apply for registration of an LPA to notify the individuals named in the LPA of your intention to register the LPA. You also require LPA002 (see appendix): Application to Register an LPA which must be sent to the Office of the Public Guardian.

If I have an LPA for Personal Welfare and an LPA for Property and Affairs will I require two different applications?
Yes, you will need a separate set of registration forms for each Power of Attorney.

Who can object to my LPA being registered?
You, your Attorney and the individuals you have selected to be notified are allowed to object to your LPA being registered.

What are the prescribed grounds for objecting to the registration of a LPA?

The prescribed grounds for objecting to the registration of a LPA are as follows:

- the Powers created by the LPA are not valid (e.g. the person objecting does not believe the Donor had capacity to make an LPA);

- the power created by LPA no longer exists (e.g. the Donor revoked it at a time when he/she had capacity to do so);

- Fraud or undue pressure was used to induce the Donor to make the LPA; or the Attorney proposes to behave in a way that would contravene his/her authority or would not be in the Donor's best interests.

Any objection that is raised will need to be supported with factual evidence.

How much does it cost to register an LPA?

The fee for registering an LPA is currently set at £130.00. The fee is payable by the person seeking to register the LPA and is recoverable from the Donor's funds. Certain individual may be entitled to exemptions or remissions of fees. For more information on fees, exemptions from fees and fee remissions go to the Office of the Public Guardian.

12

Abuse of Powers of Attorney

The function of the Court of Protection is to make sure that the person who is lacking in mental capacity has their best interests determined at all times and that there are no abuse of powers.

It has the following powers

- To make declarations as to whether a Person (P) has capacity to make a particular decision ((Mental Capacity Act 2005, section 15(1)).

- To make declarations as to the lawfulness or otherwise of an act done, or yet to be done, in relation to P (section 15 (1)(c)).

- To make single one-off orders (section 16(2)(a)), such as an order authorising the execution of a statutory will on behalf of an elderly person with Vascular dementia or Alzheimer's disease.

- To appoint a deputy to make decisions in relation to the matters in which P lacks the capacity him or herself, whether they relate to P's property and affairs or personal welfare (section 16 (2)(b)).

- To resolve various issues involving Lasting Powers of Attorney (sections 22 and 23) and Enduring Powers of Attorney (schedule 4).

- To make a declaration as to whether an advance decision to refuse treatment exists, is valid, or is applicable to a particular treatment (section 26(4)).

- To exercise an appellate jurisdiction in Deprivation of Liberty Safeguards (DOLS) cases.

What powers does it have?

The Court of Protection has the powers to:

- Decide whether a person has capacity to make a particular decision for themselves;

- Make declarations, decisions or orders on financial or welfare matters;

- Appoint deputies;

- Decide whether a Lasting Power of Attorney or Enduring Power of Attorney is valid;

- Remove deputies or attorneys who fail to carry out their duty;

- Hear cases concerning objections to register an LPA or EPA.

- But once the Court of Protection has appointed a suitable other person called a "Deputy" to act on their behalf, that Deputy will be able to take control of their bank accounts .

- They will be unfrozen and they will also be able to take control of any properties or interests to enable their sale or other transaction in the best interest of the incapable person.

- If a person does not have sufficient mental capacity to make a LPA, then a member of the family can make an application to the Court of Protection for authority to act on that person's behalf with regard to their financial affairs. Where there is no family, a professional adviser such as a solicitor or the Local Authority may make this application instead. If successful, the applicant will be appointed as that person's Deputy.

13

Revoking the Power of Attorney

The Court of Protection may confirm or revoke the registered Enduring Power of Attorney if the Donor is mentally capable of making such a revocation.

Similarly with the Lasting Power of Attorney, the dissolution or Annulment of a marriage or civil partnership will terminate the appointment of an Attorney or revoke the Power

What is a "Revocation of Power of Attorney"? Questions and answers.
A: A Revocation of Power of Attorney is a legal document signed by or on behalf of a person who granted a Power of Attorney (the Donor). It states that the donor is cancelling the powers that were given to another person (the Attorney) in an earlier Power of Attorney. The document provides written confirmation that the donor has revoked the Power of Attorney that was previously granted.

Q: Why would I want to revoke a Power of Attorney I previously granted?
A: Some reasons why you may wish to revoke a Power of Attorney include:

- The Power of Attorney is no longer necessary as you are now able to act on your own behalf;

- You no longer trust the person who is acting on your behalf (your Attorney);

- You have found a more suitable candidate to act as your Attorney;

- It is no longer practical to have your Attorney acting on your behalf (e.g. your Attorney no longer resides in the same jurisdiction as you do); and

- The purpose of the Power of Attorney has been fulfilled and you no longer need an Attorney to act for you.

Q: Is it necessary for me to have a written Revocation of Power of Attorney?

A: A Power of Attorney is a powerful legal document which can enable an Attorney to do almost anything with your property (depending on the powers you have granted in the Power of Attorney document). A revocation of a Power of Attorney is not effective against the Attorney or any third party (e.g. bank) until notice of the revocation has been received by that party. Consequently, it is a good idea to have a written document as evidence of your revocation to make sure there is no doubt as to your intention to revoke the power.

Q: When can I revoke my Power of Attorney?

A: A Power of Attorney can be revoked at any time, regardless of the termination date specified in the document, as long as the Donor is mentally capable. (Note: there are some exceptions, but these apply only to "binding" Powers of Attorney.

Q: Can I still revoke my Power of Attorney if I become incompetent?

A: An ordinary power of attorney is automatically revoked if the person who made it is found to be incompetent, but a durable/enduring power of attorney can only be revoked by the person who made it while that person is mentally competent.

Q: Do I have to specify why I am revoking my Power of Attorney?

A: You are not required to explain why you are revoking your Power of Attorney. As long as you are mentally capable, you can revoke your Power of Attorney for any reason (or for no reason).

Q. How will my Revocation of Power of Attorney become effective?

A: In order to give effect to your Revocation you must complete the following steps:

(Overleaf)

- Have your Revocation witnessed or acknowledged before a notary;

- Provide a copy of your Revocation to your Attorney and ask him/her to return all of his/her copies of the Power of Attorney;

- Provide a copy of your Revocation to any financial institutions or any other third parties where your Power of Attorney may have been used; and

- Provide a copy of your Revocation to any agency where your Power of Attorney has been recorded (e.g. County Clerk's Office, deed registry or land titles office).

14

Functions of The Office of The Public Guardian

The Office of the Public Guardian protects people who are lacking in mental capacity.

All Lasting Powers of Attorney and Enduring Powers of Attorney are registered at the OPG.

The role of the Public Guardian is to protect people who lack mental capacity to look after themselves and they do this by various means:

- By registering Lasting and Enduring Powers of Attorney

- By working with organisations such as social services, if the person is receiving social care and supervising deputies

- Making sure that the attorneys and the deputies are acting correctly and also investigating any concerns that arise

- Decide whether a power of attorney is valid and remove deputies or attorneys who fail to carry out their duties.

- The current details for access to the Office of the Public Guardian are as follows

PO Box 16185
Birmingham
B2 2WH

Emailcustomerservices@publicguardian.gsi.gov.uk
Telephone 0300 456 0300

15

Functions of The Court of Protection

What is the function of the Court of Protection?

Most of us take for granted that we have the ability to manage our own affairs, however should something happen, for example a stroke causing paralysis or an illness such as dementia, and that ability was diminished, the Court of Protection has the jurisdiction to make decisions on an affected person's behalf or appoint a suitable person to do so.

The Court of Protection has the powers to:

- Decide whether a person has capacity to make a particular decision for themselves;

- Make declarations, decisions or orders on financial or welfare matters;

- Appoint deputies;

- Decide whether an Lasting Power of Attorney or Enduring Power of Attorney is valid;

- Remove deputies or attorneys who fail to carry out their duty;

- Hear cases concerning objections to register an LPA or EPA.

What does the Court of Protection actually do?

Once a person is classed as incapable and unable to manage their financial affairs, any bank that holds monies for them may freeze their accounts. This is perfectly legal and correct and is done to prevent any third party from fraudulently operating the accounts. Or, if a person should need to move house or into residential care but is classed as mentally incapable, they are legally prevented from signing the legal paperwork in order to sell their property.

But once the Court of Protection has appointed a suitable other person called a "Deputy" to act on their behalf, that Deputy will be able to take control of their bank accounts and they will be unfrozen and they will also be able to take control of any properties or interests to enable their sale or other transaction in the best interest of the incapable person.

If that person had at some time in the past made an Enduring Power of Attorney (EPA) or Lasting Power of Attorney (LPA), then the Attorney named in that document can begin to act on the person's behalf. If that person has no EPA or LPA in place, they should take legal advice as to whether they are well enough to make a LPA. There is a strict legal test for ascertaining if a person has sufficient mental capacity to make a power of attorney. If your solicitor is unsure, they may ask for a doctor to make an assessment.

If a person does not have sufficient mental capacity to make a LPA, then a member of the family can make an application to the Court of Protection for authority to act on that person's behalf with regard to their financial affairs. Where there is no family, a professional adviser such as a solicitor or the Local Authority may make this application instead. If successful, the applicant will be appointed as that person's Deputy.

Once a Deputy is appointed, they will be able to take control of the incapable person's finances and property. The Deputy must always act in the incapable person's best interests and comply with the Mental Capacity Act 2005 and related Code of Practice. The Deputy must keep accurate records of his dealings with their assets and income and submit an annual account to the OPG. There are three levels of supervision and the Court will set this. It is also necessary for the Deputy to take out an insurance policy to cover any negligent acts.

There are prescribed application forms which must be completed to begin a Deputyship application. Notice must be given to the person's close relatives and any person with an interest in their welfare such as their unmarried partner or carer. These persons have a right to raise any concerns about the proposed Deputy's suitability to act. The Court can refuse an application by someone they consider too elderly to act or someone who has a poor history of managing their own finances. The process takes approximately six months depending on how busy the Court is. It is therefore important to consult a solicitor at an early stage if you suspect that a relative is becoming unable to manage their affairs.

It is possible for a Deputy to be appointed to make personal welfare decisions on an incapable person's behalf, e.g. where they should live or what medical treatment they should receive. However, the Court will only appoint a Deputy in extremely limited circumstances such as where there is disagreement amongst family members/carers or where their medical condition means that treatment decisions must be made frequently. Laws exist (see Section 5 of the Mental Capacity Act 2005 and the Code of Practice) to authorise the person responsible for the incapable person's care to make day-to-day personal welfare decisions on their behalf.

Aside from Deputyship decisions, applications can also be made by Attorneys or Deputies to the Court of Protection for permission to make gifts of the incapable person's assets in order to save inheritance tax or for permission to make a Will on their behalf if they should lack the ability to do so.

Joint or joint and several attorneys

With an Enduring Power of Attorney they may act jointly or jointly and severally, similarly with a Lasting Power of Attorney. If the donor fails to specify the appointment it is assumed to be jointly.

16

The Donor's Ability to Make Decisions

Under an Enduring Power of Attorney until it is registered both the Donor and the Attorney have authority to make decisions.

Once registered in theory the Donor can still make decisions.

Under a Lasting Power of Attorney the Donor can still carry on making decisions provided that they have the capacity.

With regards to personal welfare, the Attorney can make personal welfare decisions once the donor is incapable of making such decisions.

17

Registering

With and Enduring Power of Attorney, this must be registered once the Attorneys have reason to believe that the Donor has become mentally incapable.

They must however give notice to the Donor, Co-Attorneys and at least three of the Donor's relatives.

With a Lasting Power of Attorney the person named by the Donor or as being entitled to receive notification needs to be notified.

The Lasting Power of Attorney is not created until it has been registered with the Office of the Public Guardian. It cannot be used until it has been registered

The Lasting Power of Attorney can be registered at any time after the forms have been completed and signed by all those who need to sign.

The implication of not registering the Lasting Power of Attorney should be carefully considered. For example in health and welfare Lasting Power of Attorney if there was a medical emergency the attorney's would not be authorised to act until it was registered. A fee will be payable for the registration of the Lasting Power of Attorney and a separate fee for both the property and affairs under the personal welfare even if they are made by the same party.

Once registered the property and financial affairs Lasting Power of Attorney can be used while the donor still has capacity unless it is specified otherwise.

The health and welfare Lasting Power of Attorney can only be used when the donor no longer has capacity.

There is no time limit for making the application to register the Lasting Power of Attorney and it can be made by the Donor or the Attorneys. Various parties need to be notified for an application to register the Lasting Power of Attorney. If the donor decides not to include anyone to be notified then a second person will need to provide an additional certificate.

By naming a person to be notified this is a safeguard. The donor or the Attorneys making the application to register must give notice in the prescribed form to everyone named by the Donor.

The Registered Lasting Power of Attorney will be stamped on every page by the OPG. The OPG are responsible of maintaining a register of all Lasting Powers of Attorney, Enduring Powers of Attorney and Court Appointed Deputies.

A Registered Lasting Power of Attorney is a public document and will be available to anyone who applies to search the register.

18

Disclosure of the Donor's Will

There is a general duty to keep the client's affairs confidential, however the Attorney may need to know the contents of the Donor's will so as not to act contrary to the intentions of the donor, i.e. sale of an asset specifically left to someone.

The disclosure of the Donor's Will should be discussed at the time of making the Lasting Power of Attorney and instructions should be obtained.

If there is no authority the Attorney's should apply to the Court of Protections for a specific order for the contents of the Will to be disclosed

The Attorney's have a duty to keep the donor's affairs confidential including the contents of the Will.

Glossary of terms

Ability to make decisions-the donor can carry on making decisions providing he or she has the capacity to do so.

Duties of the Attorney-Statutory duties to act in accordance with the principles of the Mental Health Act best interest and with regard to the guidance of the code of practice.

Joint and Several Attorneys-where two or more persons are appointed and they must either act jointly or jointly and severally.

Lasting Power of Attorney-must be in the prescribed form.

Notification-the names of the person the donor wishes to be notified of any Application to register or must contain a Statement that there are no such persons.

Objection to Registration-the donor, the Attorney and the named person may object if the EPA is not valid or it no longer exists if the Attorneys have behaved badly.

Registering the Power-Registration can take place before the donor has lost capacity.

Registration-the Attorney cannot act under the LPA until it is registered with the Public Guardian.

Revoking the power-the donor may revoke the LPA and it may come to an end on the dissolution or annulment of marriage or civil partnership unless the instrument provider will not do so.

The Certificate provider-this is a person of the prescribed description who ensures that the donor understands the purpose of the instrument and the scope of the authority.

The Public Guardian-the office with whom the documentation needs to be registered. There are two types of Lasting Powers of Attorney:

1. Property and Financial Affairs
2. Personal Welfare including giving or refusing consent to treatment. This can only be used when the donor lacks capacity.

USEFUL CONTACTS

Age UK

Age UK
Tavis House
1-6 Tavistock Square
London WC1H 9NA

T 0800 169 2081 (general enquiries)
E contact@ageuk.org.uk
W www.ageuk.org.uk

Provides information and advice for older people in the UK. Age UK has been created by the merger of Age Concern and Help the Aged.

Alzheimer's Society

Devon House
58 St Katharine's Way
London E1W 1LB
T 020 7423 3500
E info@alzheimers.org.uk
W alzheimers.org.uk

Citizens Advice Bureau (CAB)

To find details of your nearest CAB look in the phone book, ask at your local library or consult the CAB website at www.citizensadvice.org.uk

Your local CAB is often the best starting point for advice. The service is free, confidential and independent. Most CABs have a solicitor and some have an accountant available at certain times to give free initial advice.

Court of Protection

Court of Protection
PO Box 70185
First Avenue House
42-49 High Holborn
London
WC1A 9JA

Enquiries 0300 456 4600

The Court of Protection is a specialist court for all issues relating to people who lack capacity to make specific decisions.

Office of the Public Guardian

PO Box 16185
Birmingham
B2 2WH

Email customerservices@publicguardian.gsi.gov.uk

Telephone 0300 456 0300

Customer services provide free booklets on Enduring Power of Attorney , Lasting Power of Attorney and deputyship. Their phoneline is available from 9am to 5pm on weekdays.

Solicitors for the Elderley

Sue Carraturo
SFE
Suite 209
Mill Studio Business centre
Crane Mead
Ware
Hertfordshire
SG12 9PY

0844 567 6173.
Email admin@sfe.legal

Index

Appendix

Form LPA 001 Notice of Intention to Apply for Registration of a Lasting Power of Attorney

Form LPA 002 Application to Register a Lasting power of Attorney

Form LPA114 Lasting Power of Attorney for Health and Welfare plus continuation sheets

Form LPA 117 Lasting Power of Attorney Property and Financial Affairs-plus continuation sheets.

PA 001 09.11

Notice of intention to apply for registration of a Lasting Power of Attorney

This notice must be sent to everyone named by the donor in the Lasting Power of Attorney as a person who should be notified of an application to register. Relatives are not entitled to notice unless named in the Lasting Power of Attorney.

The application to register may be made by the donor or the attorney(s).

Where attorneys are appointed to act jointly** they **all** must apply to register.

Details of the person to be told**

Name

Address

Telephone no.

Postcode

To the person to be told - You have the right to object to the proposed registration of the Lasting Power of Attorney. You have **five weeks** from the day on which this notice is given to object. Details of how to object and the grounds for doing so are on the back page.

Details of the Lasting Power of Attorney (LPA)

Who is applying to register the LPA? ☐ the donor ☐ the attorney(s)

Which type of LPA is being registered? ☐ Property and Financial Affairs ☐ Health and Welfare

(You must complete separate applications for each LPA you wish to register.)

On what date did the donor sign the LPA? | D | D | M | M | Y | Y | Y | Y |

Details of the donor

Full name

Address

Telephone no.

Postcode

© Crown copyright 2011

Details of the attorney(s)

Name of 1st attorney

Address

Telephone no.

Postcode

☐ solely   ☐ jointly and severally**

☐ jointly   ☐ jointly in some matters and jointly and severally in others

Name of 2nd attorney

Address

Telephone no.

Postcode

☐ jointly   ☐ jointly and severally

☐ jointly in some matters and jointly and severally in others

Name of 3rd attorney

Address

Telephone no.

Postcode

☐ jointly   ☐ jointly and severally

☐ jointly in some matters and jointly and severally in others

Name of 4th attorney

Address

Telephone no.

Postcode

☐ jointly   ☐ jointly and severally

☐ jointly in some matters and jointly and severally in others

Signature and date

This notice must be signed by all parties applying to register the lasting power of attorney.

Signed

Print name

Dated

D	D	M	M	Y	Y	Y	Y

How to object to the registering of a Lasting Power of Attorney (LPA)

You can ask the Office of the Public Guardian (OPG) to stop the LPA from being registered if one of the factual grounds at (A) below has occurred. You need to tell us by completing Form LPA007 which is available from the OPG and by providing evidence to accompany it. You must send us the completed LPA007 form **within five weeks** from the date this notice was given. Failure to tell us could result in the LPA being registered.

(A) Factual grounds – you can ask the Office of the Public Guardian to stop registration if:

- The Donor is bankrupt or interim bankrupt (for property and financial affairs LPAs only)
- The Attorney is bankrupt or interim bankrupt (for property and financial affairs LPAs only)
- The Attorney is a trust corporation and is wound up or dissolved (for property and financial affairs LPAs only)
- The Donor is dead
- The Attorney is dead
- That there has been dissolution or annulment of a marriage or civil partnership between the Donor and Attorney (except if the LPA provided that such an event should not affect the instrument)
- The Attorney(s) lack the capacity to be an attorney under the LPA
- The Attorney(s) have disclaimed their appointment

Form LPA007 is available from the OPG on 0300 456 0300 or www.direct.gov.uk/mentalcapacity

You have the right to object to the Court of Protection about the registration of the LPA, but only on the grounds mentioned at (B) below. To do this you must contact the Court and complete the application to object form they will send you. Using that form, you must set out your reasons for objecting. They must receive the objection within five weeks from the date this notice was given. You must also notify the OPG when you object to the Court by using the separate form LPA008 that is available to download from www.justice.gov.uk/global/forms/opg/lasting-power-of-attorney/index.htm. Failure to notify the OPG of an objection may result in registration of the LPA.

Note: If you are objecting to the appointment of a specific attorney, it may not prevent registration if other attorneys or a substitute attorney have been appointed.

(B) Prescribed grounds – you can only object to the Court of Protection against registration of the LPA on the following grounds:

- That the power purported to be created by the instrument* is not valid as a LPA. e.g. the person objecting does not believe the donor had capacity to make an LPA.
- That the power created by the instrument no longer exists e.g. the donor revoked it at a time when he/she had capacity to do so.
- That fraud or undue pressure was used to induce the donor to make the power.
- The attorney proposes to behave in a way that would contravene his authority or would not be in the donor's best interests.

Note:

* The instrument means the LPA made by the donor.

** Some of the terms used in the 2007 version of the LPA forms are different to those used in this form and in the LPA002.

'Together' means the same as 'Jointly'. 'Independently' means the same as 'Severally'.

'Named person' means the same as 'Person to be told'.

The Court will only consider objections made if they are made on the above grounds. To obtain a Court objection form please contact the Court of Protection at Archway Tower, 2 Junction Road, London N19 5SZ or Telephone 0300 456 4600.

Click here to print form

PA002 09.11 Office of the Public Guardian

Application to register a Lasting Power of Attorney

Return your completed form to:
Office of the Public Guardian
PO Box 16185
Birmingham
B2 2WH

Part 1 - The donor

Place a cross (**x**) against one option

Mr. ☐   Mrs. ☐   Ms. ☐   Miss ☐   Other ☐

If other, please specify ☐☐☐☐☐☐☐☐☐☐☐☐☐☐☐☐☐☐☐

Last name ☐☐☐☐☐☐☐☐☐☐☐☐☐☐☐☐☐☐☐☐☐☐☐☐☐

First name ☐☐☐☐☐☐☐☐☐☐☐☐☐☐☐☐☐☐☐☐☐☐☐☐☐

Middle name ☐☐☐☐☐☐☐☐☐☐☐☐☐☐☐☐☐☐☐☐☐☐☐☐☐

Address 1 ☐☐☐☐☐☐☐☐☐☐☐☐☐☐☐☐☐☐☐☐☐☐☐☐☐

Address 2 ☐☐☐☐☐☐☐☐☐☐☐☐☐☐☐☐☐☐☐☐☐☐☐☐☐

Address 3 ☐☐☐☐☐☐☐☐☐☐☐☐☐☐☐☐☐☐☐☐☐☐☐☐☐

Town/City ☐☐☐☐☐☐☐☐☐☐☐☐☐☐☐☐☐☐☐☐☐☐☐☐☐

County ☐☐☐☐☐☐☐☐☐☐☐☐☐☐☐☐☐☐☐☐☐☐☐☐☐

Postcode ☐☐☐☐☐☐☐   Daytime Tel. no. ☐☐☐☐☐☐☐   ☐☐☐☐☐☐☐☐☐

Date of birth ☐☐☐☐☐☐☐☐
D D M M Y Y Y Y

If the exact date is unknown please state the year of birth

e-mail address ☐☐☐☐☐☐☐☐☐☐☐☐☐☐☐☐☐☐☐☐☐☐☐☐☐

Please do not write below this line - For office use only

Part 2 - The persons making the application

Note: We need to know who is applying and how the attorney(s) have been appointed, please answer the questions in parts two and three carefully.

Place a cross (**x**) against one option

Is the donor applying to register the Lasting Power of Attorney?

☐ Yes

Is the attorney(s) applying to register the Lasting Power of Attorney?

☐ Yes

Part 3 - How have the attorney(s) been appointed?

The LPA states whether the attorney is to act solely, jointly or jointly and severally

Place a cross (**x**) against one option

There is only one attorney appointed

☐

There are attorneys appointed jointly and severally

☐

There are attorneys appointed jointly

☐

There are attorneys appointed jointly in some matters and jointly and severally in others

☐

Note: We need to know which, if any of the attorney(s) are making this application to register the LPA. You can tell us this by putting a cross in the box at the start of each attorney(s) details in Part 4.

Part 4 - Attorney one

Place a cross (x) in this box if attorney one is applying to register ☐

Place a cross (x) against one option

Mr. ☐ Mrs. ☐ Ms. ☐ Miss ☐ Other ☐

If other, please specify ☐☐☐☐☐☐☐☐☐☐☐☐☐☐☐☐☐

Last name ☐☐☐☐☐☐☐☐☐☐☐☐☐☐☐☐☐☐☐☐☐☐☐☐

First name ☐☐☐☐☐☐☐☐☐☐☐☐☐☐☐☐☐☐☐☐☐☐☐☐

Middle name ☐☐☐☐☐☐☐☐☐☐☐☐☐☐☐☐☐☐☐☐☐☐☐☐

Company name *(if relevant)* ☐☐☐☐☐☐☐☐☐☐☐☐☐☐☐☐☐☐☐☐☐☐☐☐

Address 1 ☐☐☐☐☐☐☐☐☐☐☐☐☐☐☐☐☐☐☐☐☐☐☐☐

Address 2 ☐☐☐☐☐☐☐☐☐☐☐☐☐☐☐☐☐☐☐☐☐☐☐☐

Address 3 ☐☐☐☐☐☐☐☐☐☐☐☐☐☐☐☐☐☐☐☐☐☐☐☐

Town/City ☐☐☐☐☐☐☐☐☐☐☐☐☐☐☐☐☐☐☐☐☐☐☐☐

County ☐☐☐☐☐☐☐☐☐☐☐☐☐☐☐☐☐☐☐☐☐☐☐☐

Postcode ☐☐☐☐☐☐☐ DX number ☐☐☐☐☐☐☐☐☐☐☐☐

Date of birth ☐☐☐☐☐☐☐☐ DX Exchange ☐☐☐☐☐☐☐☐☐☐☐☐☐☐
D D M M Y Y Y Y

Daytime Tel. no. ☐☐☐☐☐☐ ☐☐☐☐☐☐☐☐☐

Occupation ☐☐☐☐☐☐☐☐☐☐☐☐☐☐☐☐☐☐☐☐☐☐☐☐

e-mail address ☐☐☐☐☐☐☐☐☐☐☐☐☐☐☐☐☐☐☐☐☐☐☐☐

Place a cross (x) against one option that best describes your relationship to the donor

Civil partner / Spouse ☐ Child ☐ Solicitor ☐ Other ☐ Other professional ☐

If 'Other' or 'Other professional', please specify ☐☐☐☐☐☐☐☐☐☐☐☐☐☐☐

3

Part 4 - Attorney two

Place a cross (x) in this box if attorney two is applying to register ☐

Place a cross (x) against one option

Mr. ☐   Mrs. ☐   Ms. ☐   Miss ☐   Other ☐

If other, please specify

Last name

First name

Middle name

Company name *(if relevant)*

Address 1

Address 2

Address 3

Town/City

County

Postcode   DX number

Date of birth
D D M M Y Y Y Y

DX Exchange

Daytime Tel. no.

Occupation

e-mail address

Place a cross (x) against one option that best describes your relationship to the donor

Civil partner / Spouse ☐   Child ☐   Solicitor ☐   Other ☐   Other professional ☐

If 'Other' or 'Other professional', please specify

4

Part 4 - Attorney three

Place a cross (x) in this box if attorney three is applying to register ☐

Place a cross (x) against one option

Mr. ☐   Mrs. ☐   Ms. ☐   Miss ☐   Other ☐

If other, please specify ☐☐☐☐☐☐☐☐☐☐☐☐☐☐☐☐☐

Last name ☐☐☐☐☐☐☐☐☐☐☐☐☐☐☐☐☐☐☐☐☐☐☐☐

First name ☐☐☐☐☐☐☐☐☐☐☐☐☐☐☐☐☐☐☐☐☐☐☐☐

Middle name ☐☐☐☐☐☐☐☐☐☐☐☐☐☐☐☐☐☐☐☐☐☐☐☐

Company name *(if relevant)* ☐☐☐☐☐☐☐☐☐☐☐☐☐☐☐☐☐☐☐☐☐☐☐☐

Address 1 ☐☐☐☐☐☐☐☐☐☐☐☐☐☐☐☐☐☐☐☐☐☐☐☐

Address 2 ☐☐☐☐☐☐☐☐☐☐☐☐☐☐☐☐☐☐☐☐☐☐☐☐

Address 3 ☐☐☐☐☐☐☐☐☐☐☐☐☐☐☐☐☐☐☐☐☐☐☐☐

Town/City ☐☐☐☐☐☐☐☐☐☐☐☐☐☐☐☐☐☐☐☐☐☐☐☐

County ☐☐☐☐☐☐☐☐☐☐☐☐☐☐☐☐☐☐☐☐☐☐☐☐

Postcode ☐☐☐☐☐☐☐   DX number ☐☐☐☐☐☐☐☐☐☐☐☐☐

Date of birth ☐☐☐☐☐☐☐☐   DX Exchange ☐☐☐☐☐☐☐☐☐☐☐☐☐☐
D D M M Y Y Y Y

Daytime Tel. no. ☐☐☐☐☐☐☐☐   ☐☐☐☐☐☐☐☐☐☐

Occupation ☐☐☐☐☐☐☐☐☐☐☐☐☐☐☐☐☐☐☐☐☐☐☐☐

e-mail address ☐☐☐☐☐☐☐☐☐☐☐☐☐☐☐☐☐☐☐☐☐☐☐☐

Place a cross (x) against one option that best describes your relationship to the donor

Civil partner / Spouse ☐   Child ☐   Solicitor ☐   Other ☐   Other professional ☐

If 'Other' or 'Other professional', please specify ☐☐☐☐☐☐☐☐☐☐☐☐☐☐☐☐

5

Part 4 - Attorney four

Place a cross (x) in this box if attorney four is applying to register ☐

If there are additional attorneys, please provide the following details in the 'Additional information' section at the end of this form.

Place a cross (x) against one option

Mr. ☐   Mrs. ☐   Ms. ☐   Miss ☐   Other ☐

If other, please specify

Last name

First name

Middle name

Company name *(if relevant)*

Address 1

Address 2

Address 3

Town/City

County

Postcode

DX number

Date of birth
D D M M Y Y Y Y

DX Exchange

Daytime Tel. no.

Occupation

e-mail address

Place a cross (x) against one option that best describes your relationship to the donor

Civil partner / Spouse ☐   Child ☐   Solicitor ☐   Other ☐   Other professional ☐

If 'Other' or 'Other professional', please specify

6

Part 5 - Notification of people to be told

The donor or attorney(s) making the application must give notice to the people to be told nominated by the donor in the section of the LPA marked About people to be told when the application to register this lasting power of attorney is made. The date on which the notice was given **must** be completed (which is the date it was posted or given to the person to be told). If the donor decided not to notify any people to be told, please place a cross in the box provided.

The donor did not specify any people to be told in the LPA ☐

Place a cross (**x**) against one option

☐ I   ☐ We

have given notice to register in the prescribed form (LP001) to the following person(s):

Date notice given

D D M M Y Y Y Y

Last name

First name

Address 1

Address 2

Address 3

Town/City

County

Postcode

⌐Part 5 - continued

Date notice given

<table>
<tr><td>D</td><td>D</td><td>M</td><td>M</td><td>Y</td><td>Y</td><td>Y</td><td>Y</td></tr>
</table>

Last name

First name

Address 1

Address 2

Address 3

Town/City

County

Postcode

Date notice given

<table>
<tr><td>D</td><td>D</td><td>M</td><td>M</td><td>Y</td><td>Y</td><td>Y</td><td>Y</td></tr>
</table>

Last name

First name

Address 1

Address 2

Address 3

Town/City

County

Postcode

8

Part 5 - continued

Date notice given

`D D M M Y Y Y Y`

Last name

First name

Address 1

Address 2

Address 3

Town/City

County

Postcode

Date notice given

`D D M M Y Y Y Y`

Last name

First name

Address 1

Address 2

Address 3

Town/City

County

Postcode

Part 6 - Fees

Guidelines on fee exemption and remission can be obtained from the Office of the Public Guardian.

Do you wish to pay the fee by credit or debit card? ☐ Yes ☐ No

Have you enclosed a cheque for the application to register fee? ☐ Yes ☐ No

Do you wish to apply for exemption of the fee? ☐ Yes ☐ No

Do you wish to apply for remission of the fee? ☐ Yes ☐ No

If you wish to pay by credit or debit card, please provide your telephone number so an agent can call you to arrange payment when your application has been received. If you wish to apply for an exemption or remission of all or part of the fee, you must complete the separate application form available from the Office of the Public Guardian.

Part 7 - Type of power

☐ I   ☐ We

apply to register the LPA (the original of which accompanies this application) made by the donor under the provisions of the Mental Capacity Act 2005.

What type of Lasting Power of Attorney are you applying to register?

☐ Property and financial affairs   **OR**   ☐ Health and welfare

Date that the **donor** signed the Lasting Power of Attorney

☐☐☐☐☐☐☐☐
D D M M Y Y Y Y

To your knowledge, has the donor made any other Enduring Powers of Attorney or Lasting Power of Attorney? ☐ Yes ☐ No

If Yes, please give details below including registration date if applicable

Part 8 - Donor declaration

Note: This section should only be completed by the donor if they are applying for the registration of the Lasting Power of Attorney.

I apply to register the Lasting Power of Attorney (the original of which accompanies this application).

I certify that the above information is correct and that to the best of my knowledge and belief, I have completed the application in accordance with the provisions of the Mental Capacity Act 2005 and all statutory instruments made under it.

Signed _____ Date | | | | | | | | |
                                        D D M M Y Y Y Y

Last name _____

First name _____

Part 9 - Attorney(s) declaration

Note: This section should only be completed by the attorney(s) if they are applying for the registration of the Lasting Power of Attorney.

☐ I   ☐ We   apply to register the Lasting Power of Attorney (the original of which accompanies this application).

☐ I   ☐ We   certify that the above information is correct to the best of my knowledge and belief.

☐ I   ☐ We   have completed the application within the provisions of the Mental Capacity Act 2005 and all statutory instruments made under it.

Signed _____ Date | | | | | | | | |
                                        D D M M Y Y Y Y

Last name _____

First name _____

Signed _____ Date | | | | | | | | |
                                        D D M M Y Y Y Y

Last name _____

First name _____

11

Signed

Date

D D M M Y Y Y Y

Last name

First name

Signed

Date

D D M M Y Y Y Y

Last name

First name

Signed

Date

D D M M Y Y Y Y

Last name

First name

Part 10 - Declaration by a trust corporation

If you are a trust corporation making this application please complete this declaration.

☐ I ☐ We

certify that the above information is correct and that to the best of my knowledge and belief, I have completed the application in accordance with the provisions of the Mental Capacity Act 2005 and all statutory instruments made under it.

Company name

Signature of authorised person(s)

Company seal (If applicable)

Last name

First name

Part 11 - Correspondence address

Place a cross (x) against one option

Mr. ☐ Mrs. ☐ Ms. ☐ Miss ☐ Other ☐

If other, please specify ☐☐☐☐☐☐☐☐☐☐☐☐☐☐☐☐☐☐

Last name ☐☐☐☐☐☐☐☐☐☐☐☐☐☐☐☐☐☐☐☐☐☐☐☐☐☐☐☐☐☐

First name ☐☐☐☐☐☐☐☐☐☐☐☐☐☐☐☐☐☐☐☐☐☐☐☐☐☐☐☐☐☐

Middle name ☐☐☐☐☐☐☐☐☐☐☐☐☐☐☐☐☐☐☐☐☐☐☐☐☐☐☐☐☐☐

Company name ☐☐☐☐☐☐☐☐☐☐☐☐☐☐☐☐☐☐☐☐☐☐☐☐☐☐☐☐☐☐

Company reference ☐☐☐☐☐☐☐☐☐☐☐☐☐☐☐☐☐☐☐☐☐☐☐☐☐☐☐☐☐☐

Address 1 ☐☐☐☐☐☐☐☐☐☐☐☐☐☐☐☐☐☐☐☐☐☐☐☐☐☐☐☐☐☐

Address 2 ☐☐☐☐☐☐☐☐☐☐☐☐☐☐☐☐☐☐☐☐☐☐☐☐☐☐☐☐☐☐

Address 3 ☐☐☐☐☐☐☐☐☐☐☐☐☐☐☐☐☐☐☐☐☐☐☐☐☐☐☐☐☐☐

Town/City ☐☐☐☐☐☐☐☐☐☐☐☐☐☐☐☐☐☐☐☐☐☐☐☐☐☐☐☐☐☐

County ☐☐☐☐☐☐☐☐☐☐☐☐☐☐☐☐☐☐☐☐☐☐☐☐☐☐☐☐☐☐

Postcode ☐☐☐☐☐☐☐ DX number ☐☐☐☐☐☐☐☐☐☐☐☐☐☐

DX Exchange ☐☐☐☐☐☐☐☐☐☐☐☐☐☐☐☐☐☐

Daytime Tel. no. ☐☐☐☐☐☐ ☐☐☐☐☐☐☐☐☐☐

e-mail address ☐☐☐☐☐☐☐☐☐☐☐☐☐☐☐☐☐☐☐☐☐☐☐☐☐☐☐☐☐☐☐☐

13

Part 12 - Additional information

Please write down any additional information to support this application in the space below. If necessary attach additional sheets.

Thursday 19 July 2012

For OPG office use only

LPA HW
registered on

OPG reference
number

Office of the Public Guardian

Lasting power of attorney for health and welfare

About this lasting power of attorney

This lasting power of attorney allows you to choose people to act on your behalf (as an attorney) and make decisions about your **health and personal welfare**, when you are unable to make decisions for yourself. This can include decisions about your healthcare and medical treatment, decisions about where you live and day-to-day decisions about your personal welfare, such as your diet, dress or daily routine.

If you also want someone to make decisions about your **property and financial affairs**, you will need a separate form (downloadable from our website or call 0300 456 0300).

Who can fill it in?

Anyone aged 18 or over, who has the mental capacity to do so.

Before you fill in the lasting power of attorney:

1. Please read the guidance available at **direct.gov.uk/mentalcapacity** or by calling **0300 456 0300**. See, for example, the *Lasting power of attorney creation pack* or other relevant guidance booklets which are all available online or by post.

2. Make sure you understand the purpose of this lasting power of attorney and the extent of the authority you are giving your attorneys.

3. Read the separate **Information sheet** to understand all the people involved, and how the three parts of the form should be filled in.

4. Make sure you, your certificate provider(s), and your attorney(s) have read the section on page 2 called **Information you must read** before filling in their relevant part.

> **!** This lasting power of attorney could be rejected at registration if it contains any errors.

Checklist

See the information sheet for guidance on all the people involved

Part A: about you, the attorneys you are appointing, and people to be told

How many **attorneys** are you appointing? *Write in words.*

How many **replacement attorneys** are you appointing? *Write in words or write 'None' if this does not apply.*

How many **people to be told** are you choosing? *Write in words from 'None' to 'five'. If 'None' you must have two certificate providers in part B.*

Part B: about your certificate providers

How many **certificate providers** do you have? *(Tick one box)*

[ ] One   OR   [ ] Two

If you have used any continuation sheets each one must be signed and dated.
Attached to the back of this lasting power of attorney are:
(Write the number of each)

continuation sheet A1	0
continuation sheet A2	0
continuation sheet A3:HW *2 pages*	0
continuation sheet B	0
Total number of continuation sheets	0

Helpline
0300 456 0300
direct.gov.uk/mentalcapacity

Valid only with Office of the Public Guardian stamp

Information you must read

This lasting power of attorney is a legal document.

Each person who signs parts A, B and C must read this information before signing.

Purpose of this lasting power of attorney

This lasting power of attorney gives your attorneys authority to make decisions about your health and welfare when you cannot make your own decisions. This can include where you live, who visits you and the type of care you receive.

When your attorneys can act for you

Your attorneys can use this lasting power of attorney only after it has been registered and stamped on every page by the Office of the Public Guardian. **Your attorneys can only act when you lack the capacity to make the decision in question.** You may have capacity to make some decisions about your personal health and welfare but not others.

The Mental Capacity Act

Your attorneys cannot do whatever they like. They **must** follow the principles of the Mental Capacity Act 2005.

Guidance about these principles is in the Mental Capacity Act Code of Practice. Your attorneys must have regard to the Code of Practice. They can get a copy from The Stationery Office at **tso.co.uk** or read it online at **direct.gov.uk/mentalcapacity**

Principles of the Act that your attorneys must follow

1 Your attorneys must assume that you can make your own decisions unless they establish that you cannot do so.

2 Your attorneys must help you to make as many of your own decisions as you can. They cannot treat you as unable to make the decision in question unless all practicable steps to help you to do so have been made without success.

3 Your attorneys must not treat you as unable to make the decision in question simply because you make an unwise decision.

4 Your attorneys must make decisions and act in your best interests when you are unable to make the decision in question.

5 Before your attorneys make the decision in question or act for you, they must consider whether they can make the decision or act in a way that is less restrictive of your rights and freedom but still achieves the purpose.

Your best interests

Your attorneys must act in your best interests in making decisions for you when you are unable to make the decision in question yourself. They must take into account all the relevant circumstances. This includes, if appropriate, consulting you and others who are interested in your health and welfare. Any guidance you add may assist your attorneys in identifying your views.

Cancelling this lasting power of attorney

You can cancel this lasting power of attorney at any time before or after it is registered as long as you have mental capacity to cancel it. Please read the guidance available at **direct.gov.uk/ mentalcapacity**

How to fill in this form

- Tick the boxes that apply like this

- Use black or blue ink and write clearly

- Cross through any boxes or sections that don't apply to you, like this:

> Any other names you are known by in financial documents or accounts

- Don't use correction fluid – please cross out any mistakes and rewrite nearby. All corrections must be initialled by the person completing that section of the form (and their witness) like this:

> Any other names you are known by in financial
> ~~WILLIAM EDWARD SMITH~~
> A.S.B / W.E.S.   SMYTH

- Your application could be rejected if your intentions are not clear and explicit. If you are in any doubt, please start again on a new copy of the form.

What happens after you've filled it in?

The next step is to **register** it. You or your attorneys can do this at any time. The person applying will need to fill in a registration form and may need to pay a fee at that time. They will also need to send notices to the 'people to be told' named at part A when the application to register this lasting power of attorney is made. You can find out more and download the registration form at **direct.gov.uk/ mentalcapacity**

The 'people to be told' are given time to raise any concerns or objections. This means the earliest the Office of Public Guardian can register this lasting power of attorney is 6 weeks after they notify the donor or attorneys that an application to register has been received.

Your lasting power of attorney will **end** if it can no longer be used. For example, if a sole attorney dies or can no longer act for you and no replacement attorney has been named in this lasting power of attorney. Please read the guidance available at **direct.gov.uk/ mentalcapacity**

Part A Declaration by the person who is giving this lasting power of attorney

Please write clearly using black or blue ink.

1 About the person who is giving this lasting power of attorney

Mr ☐ Mrs ☐ Ms ☐ Miss ☐ Other title _____

First names

_____

Last name

_____

Date of birth

D D M M Y Y Y Y

Address and postcode

_____

Postcode _____

Any other names you are known by in medical records or welfare records

_____

2 About the attorneys you are appointing

Thinking about your attorneys

- You can appoint more than one attorney if you want to. You do not have to appoint more than one attorney.
- Each attorney must be aged 18 or over. Choose people you know and trust to make decisions for you. You are recommended to read the separate guidance for people who want to make a lasting power of attorney for health and welfare.

Your first or only attorney

Mr ☐ Mrs ☐ Ms ☐ Miss ☐ Other title _____

First names of your first or only attorney

_____

Last name of your first or only attorney

_____

Date of birth of your first or only attorney

D D M M Y Y Y Y

Address and postcode of your first or only attorney

_____

Postcode _____

📑 *If you are appointing more than two attorneys, use continuation sheet A1 to tell us about your other attorneys.*

Your second attorney
Please cross through this section if it does not apply.

Mr ☐ Mrs ☐ Ms ☐ Miss ☐ Other title _____

First names of your second attorney

_____

Last name of your second attorney

_____

Date of birth of your second attorney

D D M M Y Y Y Y

Address and postcode of your second attorney

_____

Postcode _____

Other attorneys you are appointing

Number of attorneys named in continuation sheet **A1** attached to this lasting power of attorney

_____ *Cross through this box if this does not apply*

Helpline
📞 **0300 456 0300**
🖱 direct.gov.uk/mentalcapacity

Valid only with Office of the Public Guardian stamp

3   About appointing replacements if an attorney can no longer act

Thinking about replacement attorneys

- Replacement attorneys will only act once your attorney can no longer act for you.
- You can appoint replacements to replace an attorney who does not want to act for you or who is permanently no longer able to act because they are dead, have disclaimed, lack mental capacity or if they were married to you or were your civil partner, and have now had the marriage or civil partnership annulled or dissolved.
- You do not have to appoint any replacements.
- If you appoint only one attorney and no replacements, this lasting power of attorney will end when your attorney can no longer act.

Your first or only replacement attorney   *Please cross through this section if it does not apply.*

Mr   Mrs   Ms   Miss   Other title

Date of birth of your first or only replacement

D D M M Y Y Y Y

First names of your first or only replacement

Address and postcode of your first or only replacement

Last name of your first or only replacement

Postcode

If you are appointing more than one replacement, use continuation sheet A1 to tell us about your other replacement attorneys.

Other replacement attorneys you are appointing

Number of replacement attorneys named in continuation sheet **A1** attached to this lasting power of attorney

Cross through this box if this does not apply

4 How you want your attorneys to make decisions

Thinking about how you want your attorneys to make decisions

 If you leave this section blank, your attorneys will be appointed to make all decisions jointly.

- **Jointly**: this means that the attorneys must **make all decisions together.** → *For further information on appointing your attorneys jointly, see the separate guidance.*
- **Jointly and severally**: this means that attorneys can **make decisions together and separately.** This might be useful, for example, if one attorney is not available to make a decision at a certain time. If one attorney cannot act the remaining attorney is able to continue to make decisions.
- **Jointly for some decisions, and jointly and severally for other decisions**: this means that your attorneys must make certain decisions together and may make certain decisions separately. You will need to set out below how you want this to work in practice.

Choosing which decisions must be made together and which decisions may be made separately – how this will work in practice

- Please make your intentions clear about how your attorneys are to make the decision in question, for example about where you live, who visits you and the type of care you receive.
- Please check that your intentions will work in practice – it may not be possible to register or use this lasting power of attorney if they are not workable. Please read the separate guidance for examples that will not work in practice.

How you want your attorneys to make decisions

If you are appointing only one attorney and no replacement attorneys, now go to section 5 →

Jointly	→ *Go to section 5 and cross through the box below*
Jointly and severally	→ *Go to section 5 and cross through the box below*
Jointly for some decisions, and jointly and severally for other decisions	

Only if you have ticked the last box above, now tell us in the space below which decisions your attorneys must make jointly and which decisions may be made jointly and severally

If you need more space, use continuation sheet A2

5 About life-sustaining treatment

Life-sustaining treatment means any treatment that a doctor considers necessary to keep you alive. Whether or not a treatment is life-sustaining will depend on the specific situation. Some treatments will be life-sustaining in some situations but not in others.

The decisions you authorise your attorneys to make for you in this lasting power of attorney take the place of any advance decision you have already made on the same subject.

You must be clear whether or not you want to give your attorneys this authority. This is very important so please be clear about the choice you are making. You might want to discuss this first with your attorneys or doctors and health professionals.

You must choose Option A OR Option B.

Your attorneys can **only** make decisions about life-sustaining treatment if you choose Option A. If you choose Option B, your doctors will take into account where it is practicable and appropriate the views of your attorneys and people who are interested in your welfare as well as any written statement you may have made.

When you make your choice and sign this section you **must** have a witness. If you cannot sign you can make a mark instead.

> *If you cannot sign or make a mark use continuation sheet A3:HW →*
> • someone else **must** sign for you at your direction.
> • they must sign in your presence **and** in the presence of **two witnesses.**

Option A

Do not sign both boxes

I want to give my attorneys authority to give or refuse consent to life-sustaining treatment on my behalf.

Signed in the presence of a witness by the person who is giving this lasting power of attorney

Your signature or mark

Date signed or marked

| D | D | M | M | Y | Y | Y | Y |

The date you sign (or mark) here must be the same as the date you sign or mark section 10 Declaration.

Option B

Do not sign both boxes

I do not want to give my attorneys authority to give or refuse consent to life-sustaining treatment on my behalf.

Signed in the presence of a witness by the person who is giving this lasting power of attorney

Your signature or mark

Date signed or marked

| D | D | M | M | Y | Y | Y | Y |

The date you sign (or mark) here must be the same as the date you sign or mark section 10 Declaration.

Who can be a witness

• You must be 18 or over.
• You **cannot** be an attorney or replacement attorney named at part A or any continuation sheets A to this lasting power of attorney.
• If you have been asked to be the certificate provider at part B, you can be a witness at part A.
• A person to be told when the application to register this lasting power of attorney is made can be a witness.

Witnessed by

Signature of witness

Full names of witness

Address and postcode of witness

Postcode

Helpline
0300 456 0300
direct.gov.uk/mentalcapacity

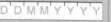 Valid only with Office of the Public Guardian stamp

6 About restrictions and conditions

Putting restrictions and conditions into words

- You should read the separate guidance for examples of conditions and restrictions that will not work in practice.
- Your attorneys **must** follow any restrictions or conditions you put in place. But it may not be possible to register or use this lasting power of attorney if a condition is not workable.
- **Either**: give any restrictions and conditions about health and welfare here
- **Or**: if you would like your attorneys to make decisions with no restrictions or conditions, you should cross through this box.

Restrictions and conditions about health and welfare

If you need more space, use continuation sheet A2

7 About guidance to your attorneys

Putting guidance into words

- Any guidance you add may help your attorneys to identify your views. You do not have to add any.
- Your attorneys do not have to follow your guidance but it will help them to understand your wishes when they make decisions for you.
- **Either**: Give any guidance about health and welfare here
- **Or**: if you have no guidance to add, please cross through this box.

Guidance to your attorneys about health and welfare

If you need more space, use continuation sheet A2

8 About paying your attorneys

Professional charges

- Professional attorneys, such as solicitors and accountants, charge for their services. You can also choose to pay a non-professional person for their services. You **should** discuss payment with your attorneys and record any agreement made here to avoid any confusion later.
- You can choose to pay non-professional attorneys for their services, but if you do not record any agreement here they will only be able to recover reasonable out-of-pocket expenses

Charges for services

If you need more space, use continuation sheet A2

→ *For further information on paying attorneys, please see the separate guidance.*

Helpline
0300 456 0300
direct.gov.uk/mentalcapacity

Valid only with Office of the Public Guardian stamp

9 About people to be told when the application to register this lasting power of attorney is made

Thinking about people to be told

- For your protection you can choose up to **five people to be told** when your lasting power of attorney is being registered. This gives people who know you well an opportunity to raise any concerns or objections **before** this lasting power of attorney is registered and can be used.

> **!** • **You do not have to choose anyone. But if you leave this section blank, you must choose two people to sign the certificate to confirm understanding at part B.**

- The people to be told cannot be your attorney or replacement named at part A or in continuation sheets to part A.

The first or only person to be told
Please cross through this section if it does not apply.

Mr   Mrs   Ms   Miss Other title
☐   ☐   ☐   ☐   _____

First names of first or only person to be told
_____

Last name of first or only person to be told
_____

Address and postcode of first or only person to be told
_____
_____
_____
Postcode _____

The second person to be told
Please cross through this section if it does not apply.

Mr   Mrs   Ms   Miss Other title
☐   ☐   ☐   ☐   _____

First names of second person to be told
_____

Last name of second person to be told
_____

Address and postcode of second person to be told
_____
_____
_____
Postcode _____

Other people to be told

Please cross through this section if it does not apply

📋 **Tell us about other people to be told on continuation sheet A1.**

Number of other people to be told named in continuation sheet **A1** attached to this lasting power of attorney

_____

10 Declaration by the person who is giving this lasting power of attorney

Before signing please check that you have:

- filled in every answer that applies to you
- crossed through blank boxes that do not apply to you
- filled in any continuation sheets
- crossed through any mistakes you have made
- initialled any changes you have made.

No changes may be made to this lasting power of attorney and no continuation sheets may be added after part A has been filled in and signed. If any change appears to have been made, this lasting power of attorney will not be valid and will be rejected when an application is made to register it.

By signing (or marking) on this page, or by directing someone to sign continuation sheet A3:HW, I confirm all of the following:

Statement of understanding

I have read or had read to me:

- the section called 'Information you must read' on page 2
- all information contained in part A and any continuation sheets to part A of this lasting power of attorney.

I appoint and give my attorneys authority to make decisions about my health and welfare, when I cannot act for myself because I lack mental capacity, subject to the terms of this lasting power of attorney and to the provisions of the Mental Capacity Act 2005.

Statement about life-sustaining treatment

I have chosen option A or option B about life-sustaining treatment in section 5 of this lasting power of attorney.

People to be told when the application to register this lasting power of attorney is made

I have chosen the people to be told, and have chosen one person to sign the certificate of understanding at part B.

OR

I do not want anyone to be told, and have chosen two people to sign certificates of understanding at part B.

If you cannot sign this lasting power of attorney you can make a mark instead.

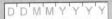 *If you cannot sign or make a mark use continuation sheet A3:HW →*

Signed (or marked) by the person giving this lasting power of attorney and delivered as a deed

Date signed or marked

 D D M M Y Y Y Y

🚫 Sign (or mark) and date
- section 5 (Option A or Option B), and
- each continuation sheet
at the same time as you sign (or mark) part A here.

You must sign (or mark) and date part A here *before* parts B and C are signed and dated.

The witness should be independent of you and:

- Must be 18 or over.
- **Cannot** be an attorney or replacement attorney named at part A or any continuation sheets to this lasting power of attorney.
- Can be a certificate provider at part B.
- Can be a person to be told when the application to register this lasting power of attorney is made.
- Must initial any changes made in Part A.

🚫 Sign section 5 (witnessing Option A or Option B) at the same time as you sign part A here.

Witnessed by
Signature of witness

Full names of witness

Address and postcode of witness

Postcode

Part B
Declaration by your first or only certificate provider: certificate to confirm understanding

Your certificate provider fills in, signs and dates this part.

Declaration by the person who is signing this certificate

Please refer to separate guidance for certificate providers. If the guidance is not followed, this lasting power of attorney may not be valid and could be rejected when an application is made to register it.

In part A (section 9) has the person giving this lasting power of attorney chosen at least one person to be told when the application to register this lasting power of attorney is made?

If yes = **one** certificate provider fills in this part

If no = the **first** certificate provider fills in this part and the **second** certificate provider must fill in continuation sheet **B** 📑.

The **donor** is the person who is giving this lasting power of attorney.

By signing below, I confirm:

My understanding of the role and responsibilities

I have read part A of this lasting power of attorney, including any continuation sheets.

I have read the section called **'Information you must read'** on page 2 of this lasting power of attorney.

I understand my role and responsibilities as a certificate provider.

Statement of acting independently

I confirm that I act independently of the attorneys and of the donor and I am aged 18 or over.

I am **not**:

- an attorney or replacement attorney named in this lasting power of attorney or any other lasting power of attorney or enduring power of attorney for the donor
- a family member related to the donor or any of their attorneys or replacements
- a business partner or paid employee of the donor or any of their attorneys or replacements
- the owner, director, manager or employee of a care home that the donor lives in, or a member of their family.

How you formed your opinion

Before signing this certificate you must establish that the donor understands what it is, the authority they are giving their attorneys, and is not being pressurised into making it.

If someone challenges this lasting power of attorney, you may need to explain how you formed your opinion.

Statement of personal knowledge or relevant professional skills

Please cross through the box that does not apply.

EITHER

I have **known** the donor for at least **two years** and as more than an acquaintance. My personal knowledge of the donor is:

OR

I have **relevant professional skills**. (Please state your profession – for example, a GP or solicitor – and then the particular skills that are relevant to you forming your opinion – for example, a consultant specialising in geriatric care.)

My profession and particular skills are:

Continues over →

Part B – Declaration by the person who is signing this certificate (continued)

Things you certify

I certify that, in my opinion, at the time of signing part A:

- the donor understands the purpose of this lasting power of attorney and the scope of the authority conferred under it
- no fraud or undue pressure is being used to induce the donor to create this lasting power of attorney
- there is nothing else which would prevent this lasting power of attorney from being created by the completion of this form.

Your signature

❗ Do not sign until part A of this lasting power of attorney has been filled in and signed.

Sign **as soon as possible** after part A is signed. If this part is signed before part A is signed, this lasting power of attorney will not be valid and will be rejected when an application is made to register it.

Signature of certificate provider

Date signed

D D M M Y Y Y Y

Name and address of the person who is signing this certificate

Mr   Mrs   Ms   Miss   Other title

First names of certificate provider

Last name of certificate provider

Address and postcode of certificate provider

Postcode

Part C Declaration by each attorney or replacement attorney

Your attorney(s) and replacement attorney(s) sign and date this part.

 If you are appointing more than one attorney, including replacement attorneys: photocopy this sheet before it is filled in so that each attorney has a copy to fill in and sign.

Statement by the attorney or replacement attorney who is signing this declaration

- Before a replacement can act for you, they must get in touch with the Office of the Public Guardian and return the original lasting power of attorney form. They will get guidance at that time about what needs to happen next.

By signing below, I confirm all of the following:

Understanding of role and responsibilities

I have read the section called 'Information you must read' on page 2 of this lasting power of attorney.

I understand my role and responsibilities under this lasting power of attorney, in particular:

- I have a duty to act based on the principles of the Mental Capacity Act 2005 and have regard to the Mental Capacity Act Code of Practice
- I can make decisions and act only when this lasting power of attorney has been registered and when the person who is giving this lasting power of attorney lacks mental capacity
- I must make decisions and act in the best interests of the person who is giving this lasting power of attorney

Further statement of replacement attorney

If an original attorney's appointment is terminated, I will replace the original attorney if I am still eligible to act as an attorney.

I have the authority to act under this lasting power of attorney only after an original attorney's appointment is terminated and I have notified the Public Guardian of the event.

! For this lasting power of attorney to be valid and registered this part should not be signed before Part A or part B have been completed, signed and dated. Sign part C **as soon as possible** after part B is signed.

Signed or marked by the attorney or replacement attorney as a deed and delivered (or if to be signed at their direction refer to separate guidance)

Full name of [attorney] or [replacement attorney] (delete as appropriate)

Date signed or marked

D D M M Y Y Y Y

The witness must be over 18 and can be:

- another attorney or replacement attorney named at part A or in continuation sheet A to this lasting power of attorney
- a certificate provider at part B of this lasting power of attorney.
- a person to be told when the application to register this lasting power of attorney is made.

The donor cannot be a witness.

The witness must see the attorney or replacement attorney sign or make a mark.

Signature of witness

Full name of witness

Address and postcode of witness to the attorney's or replacement attorney's signature

Postcode

Valid only with Office of the Public Guardian stamp

A1 Continuation sheet A1 – Additional people

Use this continuation sheet for details of all additional attorneys, replacement attorneys, or people to be told.
Make copies of this sheet before filling it in if you need more than one sheet.

About the additional people

For each additional person, provide the following details

- Whether you want them to act as an attorney, replacement attorney or person to be told

  ! If you don't make your requirements for each person clear this lasting power of attorney could be rejected at registration

- Their title, full name, address (including postcode)
- Their date of birth

For example:
- Third attorney
- Mr John Smith,
- 38 London Street, Posttown, PC6 9ZZ
- 19 January 1960

or:
- Second replacement attorney
- Mrs Susan Jones
- 27 Lincoln Road, Posttown, PC7 9XX
- 12 December 1962

About you

Name of person who is giving this lasting power of attorney

Date signed or marked

D D M M Y Y Y Y

Signed or marked by (or signed by the direction of) the person giving this lasting power of attorney

Please **attach** this sheet to the **back** of your lasting power of attorney **before** you sign and date the declaration in part A.
And number your continuation sheets consecutively.

This is continuation sheet number

Total number of continuation sheets

A2 Continuation sheet A2 – how your attorneys make decisions jointly and severally, restrictions & conditions, guidance, payment

Only use this continuation sheet to provide further additional information about how you want your attorneys to act.
Make copies of this sheet before filling it in if you need more than one sheet.

About the additional information

For each additional piece of information you are providing, state whether it relates to:

- Which decisions your attorneys should make jointly and which decisions they should make jointly and severally (only if this applies)
- Restrictions and conditions
- Guidance to your attorneys
- Paying your attorneys

About you

Name of person who is giving this lasting power of attorney

Date signed or marked

D D M M Y Y Y Y

Signed or marked by (or signed by the direction of) the person giving this lasting power of attorney

Please **attach** this sheet to the **back** of your lasting power of attorney **before** you sign and date the declaration in part A.

And number your continuation sheets consecutively.

This is continuation sheet number

Total number of continuation sheets

A3:HW Continuation sheet A3 (health and welfare) – if you cannot sign or make a mark

Use this continuation sheet if you cannot sign or make a mark at part A of your lasting power of attorney.

The person signing on behalf of the person giving this lasting power of attorney must

- sign in the person's presence **and** in the presence of **two witnesses.**
- sign in their own name
- not also be a witness.

Full name of the person signing

Option A

! Do not sign both boxes

I want to give my attorneys authority to give or refuse consent to life-sustaining treatment on my behalf.

Signature of someone signing for the person who is giving this lasting power of attorney

Date signed

D D M M Y Y Y Y

! The date you sign here must be the same as the date you sign below.

Option B

! Do not sign both boxes

I do not want to give my attorneys authority to give or refuse consent to life-sustaining treatment on my behalf.

Signature of someone signing for the person who is giving this lasting power of attorney

Date signed

D D M M Y Y Y Y

! The date you sign here must be the same as the date you sign below.

Signature of someone signing on behalf of the person giving this lasting power of attorney

I confirm that I have signed at Option A or Option B in the presence of and directed by the person giving this lasting power of attorney and in the presence of two witnesses

Date signed

D D M M Y Y Y Y

! Sign and date Option A or Option B above, and each continuation sheet, at the same time as you sign part A here.

You must sign and date part A here *before* parts B and C are signed and dated.

Signed as a deed and delivered in the presence of and directed by the person giving this lasting power of attorney and in the presence of two witnesses

📄 *This continuation sheet has two pages. Two witnesses must sign on the next page →*

Number each page individually and attach both pages of continuation sheet A3:HW to the **back** of your lasting power of attorney after they have been signed and dated.

This is continuation sheet number

Total number of continuation sheets

Continues over →

Helpline
📞 **0300 456 0300**
🖱 publicguardian.gov.uk

Valid only with Office of the Public Guardian stamp

A3:HW Continuation sheet A3 (health and welfare) – if you cannot sign or make a mark (continued)

Each witness

- Must be 18 or over.
- **Cannot** be an attorney or replacement attorney named at part A or any continuation sheets A to this lasting power of attorney.

- Can be a certificate provider at part B, .
- Can be a person to be told when the application to register this lasting power of attorney is made.
- Must initial any changes made in Part A.

Witnessed by
Signature of **first** witness

Date signed

D D M M Y Y Y Y

Full names of first witness

Address and postcode of first witness

Postcode

Also witnessed by
Signature of **second** witness

Date signed

D D M M Y Y Y Y

Full names of second witness

Address and postcode of second witness

Postcode

About you

Name of person who is giving this lasting power of attorney

📋 *This continuation sheet has two pages.*

Number each page individually and attach both pages of continuation sheet A3:HW to the **back** of your lasting power of attorney after they have been signed and dated.

This is continuation sheet number

Total number of continuation sheets

B Continuation sheet B – declaration by your second certificate provider: certificate to confirm understanding

Your second certificate provider signs and dates this continuation sheet

Declaration by the person who is signing this certificate

Please refer to separate guidance for certificate providers. If the guidance is not followed, this lasting power of attorney may not be valid and could be rejected when an application is made to register it.

In part A (property and financial affairs section 8, or health and welfare section 9) has the person giving this lasting power of attorney chosen at least one person to be told when the application to register this lasting power of attorney is made?

If yes = you only need **one** certificate provider so you do **not** need to fill in this continuation sheet

If no = the **second** certificate provider must fill in this continuation sheet

The **donor** is the person who is giving this lasting power of attorney.

By signing below, I confirm:

My understanding of the role and responsibilities

I have read part A of this lasting power of attorney, including any continuation sheets.

I have read the section called **'Information you must read'** on page 2 of this lasting power of attorney.

I understand my role and responsibilities as a certificate provider.

Statement of acting independently

I confirm that I act independently of the attorneys and of the donor and I am aged 18 or over.

I am **not**:

- an attorney or replacement attorney named in this lasting power of attorney or any other lasting power of attorney or enduring power of attorney for the donor
- a family member related to the donor or any of their attorneys or replacements
- a business partner or paid employee of the donor or any of their attorneys or replacements
- the owner, director, manager or employee of a care home that the donor lives in, or a member of their family
- a director or employee of a trust corporation appointed as an attorney or replacement attorney in this lasting power of attorney (for property and financial affairs only).

How you formed your opinion

Before signing this certificate you must establish that the donor understands what it is, the authority they are giving their attorneys, and is not being pressurised into making it.
If someone challenges this lasting power of attorney, you may need to explain how you formed your opinion.

Statement of personal knowledge or relevant professional skills

Please cross through the box that does not apply.

EITHER

I have **known** the donor for at least **two years** and as more than an acquaintance. My personal knowledge of the donor is:

OR

I have **relevant professional skills**. (Please state your profession – for example, a GP or solicitor – and then the particular skills that are relevant to you forming your opinion – for example, a consultant specialising in geriatric care'.)

My profession and particular skills are:

Number each page individually and attach both continuation sheet B pages to the back of your lasting power of attorney **after** you sign and date the declaration in part A.

This is continuation sheet number [ ]

Total number of continuation sheets [ ]

Continues over →

B Continuation sheet B (continued) – declaration by your second certificate provider: certificate to confirm understanding

Declaration by the person who is signing this certificate (continued)

Things you certify

I certify that, in my opinion, at the time of signing part A:

- the donor understands the purpose of this lasting power of attorney and the scope of the authority conferred under it
- no fraud or undue pressure is being used to induce the donor to create this lasting power of attorney
- there is nothing else which would prevent this lasting power of attorney from being created by the completion of this form.

Your signature

🚫 **Do not sign until part A of this lasting power of attorney has been filled in and signed.**

Sign **as soon as possible** after part A is signed. If this part is signed before part A is signed, this lasting power of attorney will not be valid and will be rejected when an application is made to register it.

Signature of certificate provider

Date signed

D D M M Y Y Y Y

Name and address of the person who is signing this certificate

Mr ☐ Mrs ☐ Ms ☐ Miss ☐ Other title _____

First names of certificate provider

Last name of certificate provider

Address and postcode of certificate provider

Postcode

Number each page individually and attach both pages of continuation sheet B to the back of your lasting power of attorney **after** you sign and date the declaration in part A.

This is continuation sheet number _____

Total number of continuation sheets _____

Thursday 19 July 2012

For OPG office use only

| LPA PA registered on | |
| OPG reference number | |

Office of the Public Guardian

Lasting power of attorney – property and financial affairs

About this lasting power of attorney

This lasting power of attorney allows you to choose people to act on your behalf (as an attorney) and make decisions about your **property and financial affairs**, when you are unable to make decisions for yourself.

If you also want someone to make decisions about your **health and welfare**, you will need a separate form (downloadable from our website or call 0300 456 0300).

Who can fill it in?

Anyone aged 18 or over, who has the mental capacity to do so.

Before you fill in the lasting power of attorney:

1. Please read the guidance available at **direct.gov.uk/mentalcapacity** or by calling **0300 456 0300**. See, for example, the *Guidance for people who want to make a lasting power of attorney for property and financial affairs* or other relevant guidance booklets which are all available online or by post.

2. Make sure you understand the purpose of this lasting power of attorney and the extent of the authority you are giving your attorneys.

3. Read the separate **Information sheet** to understand all the people involved, and how the three parts of the form should be filled in.

4. Make sure you, your certificate provider(s), and your attorney(s) have read the section on page 2 called **Information you must read** before filling in their relevant part.

> **!** This lasting power of attorney could be rejected at registration if it contains any errors.

Checklist

See the information sheet for guidance on all the people involved

Part A: about you, the attorneys you are appointing, and people to be told

How many **attorneys** are you appointing? *Write in words.*

[ ]

How many **replacement attorneys** are you appointing? *Write in words or write 'None' if this does not apply.*

[ ]

How many **people to be told** are you choosing? *Write in words from 'None' to 'five'. If 'None' you must have two certificate providers in part B.*

[ ]

Part B: about your certificate providers

How many **certificate providers** do you have? *(Tick one box)*

[ ] One   OR   [ ] Two

If you have used any continuation sheets each one must be signed and dated.
Attached to the back of this lasting power of attorney are:
(Write the number of each)

continuation sheet A1	0
continuation sheet A2	0
continuation sheet A3:PFA	0
continuation sheet B	0
continuation sheet C	0
Total number of continuation sheets	0

Helpline
0300 456 0300
direct.gov.uk/mentalcapacity

Information you must read

This lasting power of attorney is a legal document.

Each person who signs parts A, B and C must read this information before signing.

Purpose of this lasting power of attorney

This lasting power of attorney gives your attorneys authority to make decisions about your property and financial affairs when you cannot make your own decisions. This can include running your bank accounts and savings accounts, decisions about making or selling investments and selling property, and spending your money.

When your attorneys can act for you

Your attorneys can use this lasting power of attorney only after it has been registered and stamped on every page by the Office of the Public Guardian. Your attorneys can make decisions for you as soon as this lasting power of attorney is registered – both when you have mental capacity and when you lack mental capacity, unless you put a restriction in this lasting power of attorney.

The Mental Capacity Act

Your attorneys cannot do whatever they like. They **must** follow the principles of the Mental Capacity Act 2005.

Guidance about these principles is in the Mental Capacity Act Code of Practice. Your attorneys must have regard to the Code of Practice. They can get a copy from The Stationery Office at **tso.co.uk** or read it online at **direct.gov.uk/mentalcapacity**

Principles of the Act that your attorneys must follow

1 Your attorneys must assume that you can make your own decisions unless they establish that you cannot do so.

2 Your attorneys must help you to make as many of your own decisions as you can. They cannot treat you as unable to make the decision in question unless all practicable steps to help you to do so have been made without success.

3 Your attorneys must not treat you as unable to make the decision in question simply because you make an unwise decision.

4 Your attorneys must make decisions and act in your best interests when you are unable to make the decision in question.

5 Before your attorneys make the decision in question or act for you, they must consider whether they can make the decision or act in a way that is less restrictive of your rights and freedom but still achieves the purpose.

Your best interests

Your attorneys must act in your best interests in making decisions for you when you are unable to make the decision yourself. They must take into account all the relevant circumstances. This includes, if appropriate, consulting you and others who are interested in your welfare. Any guidance you add may assist your attorneys in identifying your views.

Cancelling this lasting power of attorney

You can cancel this lasting power of attorney at any time before or after it is registered as long as you have mental capacity to cancel it. Please read the guidance available at **direct.gov.uk/mentalcapacity**

How to fill in this form

- Tick the boxes that apply like this $\boxed{\checkmark}$

- Use black or blue ink and write clearly

- Cross through any boxes or sections that don't apply to you, like this:

- Don't use correction fluid – please cross out any mistakes and rewrite nearby. All corrections must be initialled by the person completing that section of the form (and their witness) like this:

Any other names you are known by in financial documents or accounts

~~WILLIAM EDWARD SMITH~~   *A.S.B / W.E.S.*   SMYTH

- Your application could be rejected if your intentions are not clear and explicit. If you are in any doubt, please start again on a new copy of the form.

What happens after you've filled it in?

The next step is to **register** it. You or your attorneys can do this at any time. The person applying will need to fill in a registration form and may need to pay a fee at that time. They will also need to send notices to the 'people to be told' named at part A when the application to register this lasting power of attorney is made. You can find out more and download the registration form at **direct.gov.uk/ lparegistration**

The 'people to be told' are given time to raise any concerns or objections. This means the earliest the Office of Public Guardian can register this lasting power of attorney is 6 weeks after they notify the donor or attorneys that an application to register has been received.

Your lasting power of attorney will **end** if it can no longer be used. For example, if a sole attorney dies or can no longer act for you and no replacement attorney has been named in this lasting power of attorney. Please read the guidance available at **direct.gov.uk/ mentalcapacity**

Part A Declaration by the person who is giving this lasting power of attorney

Please write clearly using black or blue ink.

1 About the person who is giving this lasting power of attorney

Mr ☐   Mrs ☐   Ms ☐   Miss ☐   Other title [ ]

First names

[ ]

Last name

[ ]

Date of birth

[D D M M Y Y Y Y]

Address and postcode

[ ]

Postcode [ ]

Any other names you are known by in financial documents or accounts

[ ]

2 About the attorneys you are appointing

📋 *If you are appointing a trust corporation alone, cross through this section and go to 2A →*

Thinking about your attorneys

- You can appoint more than one attorney if you want to. You do not have to appoint more than one attorney.
- Each attorney must be aged 18 or over. Choose people you know and trust to make decisions for you. You are recommended to read the separate guidance for people who want to make a lasting power of attorney for property and financial affairs.
- Your attorney must not be bankrupt.

Your first or only attorney

Mr ☐   Mrs ☐   Ms ☐   Miss ☐   Other title [ ]

First names of your first or only attorney

[ ]

Last name of your first or only attorney

[ ]

Date of birth of your first or only attorney

[D D M M Y Y Y Y]

Address and postcode of your first or only attorney

[ ]

Postcode [ ]

Your second attorney
Please cross through this section if it does not apply.

Mr ☐   Mrs ☐   Ms ☐   Miss ☐   Other title [ ]

First names of your second attorney

[ ]

Last name of your second attorney

[ ]

Date of birth of your second attorney

[D D M M Y Y Y Y]

Address and postcode of your second attorney

[ ]

Postcode [ ]

📋 *If you are appointing more than two attorneys, use continuation sheet A1 to tell us about your other attorneys.*

Other attorneys you are appointing

Number of attorneys named in continuation sheet **A1** attached to this lasting power of attorney

[ ]   *Cross through this box if this does not apply*

Helpline
📞 **0300 456 0300**
🖱 direct.gov.uk/mentalcapacity

Valid only with Office of the Public Guardian stamp

2A About appointing a trust corporation as attorney or replacement attorney

About the trust corporation you are appointing *Please cross through this section if it does not apply.*
- A trust corporation cannot be going through winding-up proceedings.

Company name

Address

Are you appointing this trust corporation to act as an

☐ attorney, or

☐ replacement attorney?

Postcode

3 About appointing replacements if an attorney can no longer act

If you are appointing a trust corporation as replacement attorney, cross through this section.
Your trust corporation should then fill in continuation sheet C →

Thinking about replacement attorneys
- Replacement attorneys will only act once your attorney can no longer act for you.
- You can appoint replacements to replace an attorney who does not want to act for you or who is permanently no longer able to act because they are dead, bankrupt, have disclaimed, lack mental capacity or if they were married to you or were your civil partner, and have now had the marriage or civil partnership annulled or dissolved.
- You do not have to appoint any replacements.
- If you appoint only one attorney and no replacements, this lasting power of attorney will end when your attorney can no longer act.

Your first or only replacement attorney *Please cross through this section if it does not apply.*

Mr ☐ Mrs ☐ Ms ☐ Miss ☐ Other title

Date of birth of your first or only replacement

D D M M Y Y Y Y

First names of your first or only replacement

Address and postcode of your first or only replacement

Last name of your first or only replacement

Postcode

If you are appointing more than one replacement, use continuation sheet A1 to tell us about your other replacement attorneys.

Other replacement attorneys you are appointing

Number of replacement attorneys named in continuation sheet **A1** attached to this lasting power of attorney

Cross through this box if this does not apply

4 How you want your attorneys to make decisions

Thinking about how you want your attorneys to make decisions

 If you leave this section blank, your attorneys will be appointed to make all decisions jointly.

- **Jointly**: this means that the attorneys must **make all decisions together.** → *For further information on appointing your attorneys jointly, see the separate guidance.*

- **Jointly and severally**: this means that attorneys can make decisions together and separately. This might be useful, for example, if one attorney is not available to make a decision at a certain time. If one attorney cannot act the remaining attorney is able to continue to make decisions.

- **Jointly for some decisions, and jointly and severally for other decisions**: this means that your attorneys **must make certain decisions together** and **may make certain decisions separately.** You will need to set out below how you want this to work in practice.

Choosing which decisions must be made together and which decisions may be made separately – how this will work in practice

- Please make your intentions clear about how your attorneys are to make decisions about running bank accounts and savings accounts, making or selling investments and selling property, and spending your money.

- Please check that your intentions will work in practice – it may not be possible to register or use this lasting power of attorney if, for example, a bank or building society account cannot be operated as you wish.

How you want your attorneys to make decisions

If you are appointing only one attorney and no replacement attorneys, now go to section 5 →

Jointly	☐	*→ Go to section 5 and cross through the box below*
Jointly and severally	☐	*→ Go to section 5 and cross through the box below*
Jointly for some decisions, and jointly and severally for other decisions	☐	

Only if you have ticked the last box above, now tell us in the space below which decisions your attorneys must make jointly and which decisions may be made jointly and severally

If you need more space, use continuation sheet A2

5 About restrictions and conditions

Putting restrictions and conditions into words

- You should read the separate guidance for examples of conditions and restrictions that will not work in practice.
- Your attorneys **must** follow any restrictions or conditions you put in place. But it may not be possible to register or use this lasting power of attorney if a condition is not workable.
- **Either**: give any restrictions and conditions about property and financial affairs here
- **Or**: if you would like your attorneys to make decisions with no restrictions or conditions, you should cross through this box.

Restrictions and conditions about property and financial affairs

If you need more space, use continuation sheet A2

6 About guidance to your attorneys

Putting guidance into words

- Any guidance you add may help your attorneys to identify your views. You do not have to add any.
- Your attorneys do not have to follow your guidance but it will help them to understand your wishes when they make decisions for you.
- **Either**: Give any guidance about property and financial affairs here
- **Or**: if you have no guidance to add, please cross through this box.

Guidance to your attorneys about property and financial affairs

If you need more space, use continuation sheet A2

7 About paying your attorneys

Professional charges

- Professional attorneys, such as solicitors and accountants, charge for their services. You can also choose to pay a non-professional person for their services. You **should** discuss payment with your attorneys and record any agreement made here to avoid any confusion later.
- You can choose to pay non-professional attorneys for their services, but if you do not record any agreement here they will only be able to recover reasonable out-of-pocket expenses

Charges for services

If you need more space, use continuation sheet A2

→ *For further information on paying attorneys, please see the separate guidance.*

Helpline
0300 456 0300
direct.gov.uk/mentalcapacity

Valid only with Office of the Public Guardian stamp

8 About people to be told when the application to register this lasting power of attorney is made

Thinking about people to be told

- For your protection you can choose up to **five people to be told** when your lasting power of attorney is being registered. This gives people who know you well an opportunity to raise any concerns or objections **before** this lasting power of attorney is registered and can be used.

> **❶** • You do not have to choose anyone. But if you leave this section blank, you must choose two people to sign the certificate to confirm understanding at part B.

- The people to be told cannot be your attorney or replacement named at part A or in continuation sheets to part A.

The first or only person to be told	The second person to be told
Please cross through this section if it does not apply.	*Please cross through this section if it does not apply.*

The first or only person to be told
Please cross through this section if it does not apply.

Mr ☐ Mrs ☐ Ms ☐ Miss ☐ Other title _____

First names of first or only person to be told
_____

Last name of first or only person to be told
_____

Address and postcode of first or only person
to be told
_____

Postcode _____

The second person to be told
Please cross through this section if it does not apply.

Mr ☐ Mrs ☐ Ms ☐ Miss ☐ Other title _____

First names of second person to be told
_____

Last name of second person to be told
_____

Address and postcode of second person
to be told
_____

Postcode _____

Other people to be told

Please cross through this section if it does not apply

📄 *Tell us about other people to be told on continuation sheet A1.*

Number of other people to be told named in continuation
sheet **A1** attached to this lasting power of attorney
_____

9 Declaration by the person who is giving this lasting power of attorney

Before signing please check that you have:

- filled in every answer that applies to you
- crossed through blank boxes that do not apply to you
- filled in any continuation sheets
- crossed through any mistakes you have made
- initialled any changes you have made.

No changes may be made to this lasting power of attorney and no continuation sheets may be added after part A has been filled in and signed. If any change appears to have been made, this lasting power of attorney will not be valid and will be rejected when an application is made to register it.

By signing (or marking) on this page, or by directing someone to sign continuation sheet A3:PFA, I confirm all of the following:

Statement of understanding

I have read or had read to me:

- **the section called 'Information you must read' on page 2**
- **all information contained in part A and any continuation sheets to part A of this lasting power of attorney.**

I appoint and give my attorneys authority to make decisions about my property and financial affairs, including when I cannot act for myself because I lack mental capacity, subject to the terms of this lasting power of attorney and to the provisions of the Mental Capacity Act 2005.

People to be told when the application to register this lasting power of attorney is made

I have chosen the people to be told, and have chosen **one** person to sign the certificate of understanding at part B.

OR

I do not want anyone to be told, and have chosen **two** people to sign certificates of understanding at part B.

If you cannot sign this lasting power of attorney you can make a mark instead.

 If you cannot sign or make a mark use continuation sheet A3:PFA →

Signed (or marked) by the person giving this lasting power of attorney and delivered as a deed

Sign with usual signature

Date signed or marked

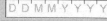 D D M M Y Y Y Y

🛈 Sign (or mark) and date each continuation sheet at the same time as you sign (or mark) part A.

You must sign (or mark) and date part A here *before* parts B and C are signed and dated.

The witness should be independent of you and:

- Must be 18 or over.
- **Cannot** be an attorney or replacement attorney named at part A or any continuation sheets to this lasting power of attorney or the employee of any trust corporation named as an attorney or replacement attorney.
- Can be a certificate provider at part B.
- Can be a person to be told when the application to register this lasting power of attorney is made.
- Must initial any changes made in Part A.

Witnessed by

Signature of witness

Full names of witness

Address and postcode of witness

Postcode

Part B
Declaration by your first or only certificate provider: certificate to confirm understanding

Your certificate provider fills in, signs and dates this part.

Declaration by the person who is signing this certificate

Please refer to separate guidance for certificate providers. If the guidance is not followed, this lasting power of attorney may not be valid and could be rejected when an application is made to register it.

In part A (section 8) has the person giving this lasting power of attorney chosen at least one person to be told when the application to register this lasting power of attorney is made?

If yes = **one** certificate provider fills in this part

If no = the **first** certificate provider fills in this part and the **second** certificate provider must fill in continuation sheet B 📄.

The **donor** is the person who is giving this lasting power of attorney.

By signing below, I confirm:

My understanding of the role and responsibilities

I have read part A of this lasting power of attorney, including any continuation sheets.

I have read the section called '**Information you must read**' on page 2 of this lasting power of attorney.

I understand my role and responsibilities as a certificate provider.

Statement of acting independently

I confirm that I act independently of the attorneys and of the donor and I am aged 18 or over.

I am **not**:

- an attorney or replacement attorney named in this lasting power of attorney or any other lasting power of attorney or enduring power of attorney for the donor
- a family member related to the donor or any of their attorneys or replacements
- a business partner or paid employee of the donor or any of their attorneys or replacements
- the owner, director, manager or employee of a care home that the donor lives in, or a member of their family
- a director or employee of a trust corporation appointed as an attorney or replacement attorney in this lasting power of attorney.

How you formed your opinion

Before signing this certificate you must establish that the donor understands what it is, the authority they are giving their attorneys, and is not being pressurised into making it.

If someone challenges this lasting power of attorney, you may need to explain how you formed your opinion.

Statement of personal knowledge or relevant professional skills

Please cross through the box that does not apply.

EITHER

I have **known** the donor for at least **two years** and as more than an acquaintance. My personal knowledge of the donor is:

OR

I have **relevant professional skills**. (Please state your profession – for example, a GP or solicitor – and then the particular skills that are relevant to you forming your opinion – for example, a consultant specialising in geriatric care.)

My profession and particular skills are:

Continues over →

Part B – Declaration by the person who is signing this certificate (continued)

Things you certify

I **certify** that, in my opinion, at the time of signing part A:

- the donor understands the purpose of this lasting power of attorney and the scope of the authority conferred under it
- no fraud or undue pressure is being used to induce the donor to create this lasting power of attorney
- there is nothing else which would prevent this lasting power of attorney from being created by the completion of this form.

Your signature

> **Do not sign until part A of this lasting power of attorney has been filled in and signed.**
>
> Sign **as soon as possible** after part A is signed. If this part is signed before part A is signed, this lasting power of attorney will not be valid and will be rejected when an application is made to register it.

Signature of certificate provider

Date signed

D D M M Y Y Y Y

Name and address of the person who is signing this certificate

Mr   Mrs   Ms   Miss   Other title

First names of certificate provider

Last name of certificate provider

Address and postcode of certificate provider

Postcode

Part C

Declaration by each attorney or replacement attorney
Your attorney(s) and replacement attorney(s) sign and date this part.

📋 *If you are appointing more than one attorney, including replacement attorneys: photocopy this sheet before it is filled in so that each attorney has a copy to fill in and sign.*

Statement by the attorney or replacement attorney who is signing this declaration

- The attorney or replacement attorney must not be bankrupt.
- Before a replacement can act for you, they must get in touch with the Office of the Public Guardian and return the original lasting power of attorney form. They will get guidance at that time about what needs to happen next.

By signing below, I confirm all of the following:

Understanding of role and responsibilities

I have read the section called 'Information you must read' on page 2 of this lasting power of attorney.

I understand my role and responsibilities under this lasting power of attorney, in particular:

- I have a duty to act based on the principles of the Mental Capacity Act 2005 and have regard to the Mental Capacity Act Code of Practice
- I can make decisions and act only when this lasting power of attorney has been registered
- I must make decisions and act in the best interests of the person who is giving this lasting power of attorney
- I can spend money to make gifts but only to charities or on customary occasions and for reasonable amounts
- I have a duty to keep accounts and financial records and produce them to the Office of the Public Guardian and/or to the Court of Protection on request.

Further statement of replacement attorney

If an original attorney's appointment is terminated, I will replace the original attorney if I am still eligible to act as an attorney.

I have the authority to act under this lasting power of attorney only after an original attorney's appointment is terminated and I have notified the Public Guardian of the event.

> ❗ **For this lasting power of attorney to be valid and registered this part should not be signed before Part A or part B have been completed, signed and dated. Sign part C as soon as possible** after part B is signed.

Signed or marked by the attorney or replacement attorney as a deed and delivered (or if to be signed at their direction refer to separate guidance)

Full name of [attorney] or [replacement attorney]
delete as appropriate

Date signed or marked

D D M M Y Y Y Y

The witness must be over 18 and can be:

- another attorney or replacement attorney named at part A or in continuation sheet A to this lasting power of attorney.
- a certificate provider at part B of this lasting power of attorney.
- a person to be told when the application to register this lasting power of attorney is made.

The donor cannot be a witness.

The witness must see the attorney or replacement attorney sign or make a mark.

Signature of witness

Full name of witness

Address and postcode of witness

Postcode

Helpline
0300 456 0300
direct.gov.uk/mentalcapacity

Valid only with Office of the Public Guardian stamp

A1 Continuation sheet A1 – Additional people

Use this continuation sheet for details of all additional attorneys, replacement attorneys, or people to be told.
Make copies of this sheet before filling it in if you need more than one sheet.

About the additional people

For each additional person, provide the following details

- Whether you want them to act as an attorney, replacement attorney or person to be told

> ! If you don't make your requirements for each person clear this lasting power of attorney could be rejected at registration

- Their title, full name, address (including postcode)
- Their date of birth

For example:
- Third attorney
- Mr John Smith,
- 38 London Street, Posttown, PC6 9ZZ
- 19 January 1960

or:
- Second replacement attorney
- Mrs Susan Jones
- 27 Lincoln Road, Posttown, PC7 9XX
- 12 December 1962

About you

Name of person who is giving this lasting power of attorney

Signed or marked by (or signed by the direction of) the person giving this lasting power of attorney

Date signed or marked

D D M M Y Y Y Y

Please **attach** this sheet to the **back** of your lasting power of attorney **before** you sign and date the declaration in part A.

And number your continuation sheets consecutively.

This is continuation sheet number

Total number of continuation sheets

Helpline
☎ **0300 456 0300**
direct.gov.uk/mentalcapacity

Valid only with Office of the Public Guardian stamp

LPA118 (09.11)

© Crown copyright 2011

A2 Continuation sheet A2 – how your attorneys make decisions jointly and severally, restrictions & conditions, guidance, payment

Only use this continuation sheet to provide further additional information about how you want your attorneys to act. Make copies of this sheet before filling it in if you need more than one sheet.

About the additional information

For each additional piece of information you are providing, state whether it relates to:

- Which decisions your attorneys should make jointly and which decisions they should make jointly and severally (only if this applies)
- Restrictions and conditions
- Guidance to your attorneys
- Paying your attorneys

About you

Name of person who is giving this lasting power of attorney

Signed or marked by (or signed by the direction of) the person giving this lasting power of attorney

Date signed or marked

D D M M Y Y Y Y

Please **attach** this sheet to the **back** of your lasting power of attorney **before** you sign and date the declaration in part A.

And number your continuation sheets consecutively.

This is continuation sheet number

Total number of continuation sheets

A3:PFA Continuation sheet A3 (property and financial affairs) – if you cannot sign or make a mark

Use this continuation sheet if you cannot sign at part A of your lasting power of attorney.

Signature of someone signing on behalf of the person giving this lasting power of attorney

The person signing on behalf of the person giving this lasting power of attorney must

- sign in the person's presence **and** in the presence of **two witnesses.**
- sign in their own name
- not also be a witness.

Full name of the person signing

! **Sign and date each continuation sheet at the same time as you sign part A here**

You must sign and date part A here *before* parts B and C are signed and dated.

Signed as a deed and delivered in the presence of and at the direction of the person giving this lasting power of attorney and in the presence of two witnesses

Date signed

D D M M Y Y Y Y

Each witness

- Must be 18 or over
- **Cannot** be an attorney or replacement attorney named at part A or any continuation sheet A to this lasting power of attorney

- Can be a certificate provider at part B
- Can be a person to be told when the application to register this lasting power of attorney is made
- Must initial any changes made in Part A

Witnessed by
Signature of **first** witness

Date signed

D D M M Y Y Y Y

Full names of first witness

Address and postcode of first witness

Postcode

Also witnessed by
Signature of **second** witness

Date signed

D D M M Y Y Y Y

Full names of second witness

Address and postcode of second witness

Postcode

About you

Name of person who is giving this lasting power of attorney

Please **attach** to the **back** of your lasting power of attorney after this sheet has been signed and dated.
And number your continuation sheets consecutively.

This is continuation sheet number

Total number of continuation sheets

Helpline
0300 456 0300
direct.gov.uk/mentalcapacity

Valid only with Office of the Public Guardian stamp

B Continuation sheet B – declaration by your second certificate provider: certificate to confirm understanding

Your second certificate provider signs and dates this continuation sheet

Declaration by the person who is signing this certificate

Please refer to separate guidance for certificate providers. If the guidance is not followed, this lasting power of attorney may not be valid and could be rejected when an application is made to register it.

In part A (property and financial affairs section 8, or health and welfare section 9) has the person giving this lasting power of attorney chosen at least one person to be told when the application to register this lasting power of attorney is made?

If yes = you only need **one** certificate provider so you do **not** need to fill in this continuation sheet

If no = the **second** certificate provider must fill in this continuation sheet

The **donor** is the person who is giving this lasting power of attorney.

By signing below, I confirm:

My understanding of the role and responsibilities

I have read part A of this lasting power of attorney, including any continuation sheets.

I have read the section called **'Information you must read'** on page 2 of this lasting power of attorney.

I understand my role and responsibilities as a certificate provider.

Statement of acting independently

I confirm that I act independently of the attorneys and of the donor and I am aged 18 or over.

I am **not**:

- an attorney or replacement attorney named in this lasting power of attorney or any other lasting power of attorney or enduring power of attorney for the donor
- a family member related to the donor or any of their attorneys or replacements
- a business partner or paid employee of the donor or any of their attorneys or replacements
- the owner, director, manager or employee of a care home that the donor lives in, or a member of their family
- a director or employee of a trust corporation appointed as an attorney or replacement attorney in this lasting power of attorney (for property and financial affairs only).

How you formed your opinion

Before signing this certificate you must establish that the donor understands what it is, the authority they are giving their attorneys, and is not being pressurised into making it.

If someone challenges this lasting power of attorney, you may need to explain how you formed your opinion.

Statement of personal knowledge or relevant professional skills

Please cross through the box that does not apply.

EITHER

I have **known** the donor for at least **two years** and as more than an acquaintance. My personal knowledge of the donor is:

OR

I have **relevant professional skills**. (Please state your profession – for example, a GP or solicitor – and then the particular skills that are relevant to you forming your opinion – for example, a consultant specialising in geriatric care'.)

My profession and particular skills are:

Number each page individually and attach both continuation sheet B pages to the back of your lasting power of attorney **after** you sign and date the declaration in part A.

This is continuation sheet number

Total number of continuation sheets

Continues over →

Helpline
0300 456 300
direct.gov.uk/mentalcapacity

Valid only with Office of the Public Guardian stamp

B Continuation sheet B (continued) – declaration by your second certificate provider: certificate to confirm understanding

Declaration by the person who is signing this certificate (continued)

Things you certify

I **certify** that, in my opinion, at the time of signing part A:

- the donor understands the purpose of this lasting power of attorney and the scope of the authority conferred under it
- no fraud or undue pressure is being used to induce the donor to create this lasting power of attorney
- there is nothing else which would prevent this lasting power of attorney from being created by the completion of this form.

Your signature

❗ Do not sign until part A of this lasting power of attorney has been filled in and signed.

Sign **as soon as possible** after part A is signed. If this part is signed before part A is signed, this lasting power of attorney will not be valid and will be rejected when an application is made to register it.

Signature of certificate provider

Date signed

D D M M Y Y Y Y

Number each page individually and attach both pages of continuation sheet B to the back of your lasting power of attorney **after** you sign and date the declaration in part A.

Name and address of the person who is signing this certificate

Mr   Mrs   Ms   Miss   Other title

First names of certificate provider

Last name of certificate provider

Address and postcode of certificate provider

Postcode

This is continuation sheet number

Total number of continuation sheets

C Continuation sheet C – appointing a trust corporation as attorney or replacement attorney

Use this continuation sheet if you are appointing a trust corporation as attorney or replacement attorney.

A trust corporation cannot be going through winding-up proceedings.

Statement by the trust corporation acting as attorney or replacement attorney – person(s) signing on behalf of the trust corporation sign and date this statement

By execution of this deed the trust corporation confirms all of the following:

Understanding of role and responsibilities

It has read the section called 'Information you must read' on page 2 of this lasting power of attorney.

It understands its role and responsibilities under this lasting power of attorney, in particular it:

- has a duty to act based on the legal principles of the Mental Capacity Act 2005 and have regard to the Mental Capacity Act Code of Practice
- can make decisions and act only when this lasting power of attorney has been registered
- must make decisions and act in the best interests of the person who is giving this lasting power of attorney
- can spend money to make gifts but only to charities or on customary occasions and for reasonable amounts
- has a duty to keep accounts and financial records and produce them to the Office of the Public Guardian or the Court of Protection on request.

Tick the option which applies:

Either:

☐ Seal of trust corporation stamped below

Or:

☐ At least one authorised person has signed and dated in the right-hand column

> **!** For this lasting power of attorney to be valid and registered this part should not be signed before Part A or part B have been completed, signed and dated. Sign part C **as soon as possible** after part B is signed.

I/We are authorised to sign on behalf of the trust corporation acting as attorney whose details are given in this continuation sheet to this lasting power of attorney.

Signed as a deed and delivered by

Signature of first authorised person

Full name of first person signing

Date signed

D D M M Y Y Y Y

Signature of second authorised person (*cross through if only one authorised person is required*)

Full name of second person signing

Date signed

D D M M Y Y Y Y

Company registration number

Please **attach** this sheet to the **back** of your lasting power of attorney **after** parts A and B are signed.

And number your continuation sheets consecutively.

This is continuation sheet number ☐

Total number of continuation sheets ☐

Emerald Publishing
www.emeraldpublishing.co.uk

Other titles in the Emerald Series:

Law
Guide to Bankruptcy
Conducting Your Own Court case
Guide to Consumer law
Creating a Will
Guide to Family Law
Guide to Employment Law
Guide to European Union Law
Guide to Health and Safety Law
Guide to Criminal Law
Guide to Landlord and Tenant Law
Guide to the English Legal System
Guide to Housing Law
Guide to Marriage and Divorce
Guide to The Civil Partnerships Act
Guide to The Law of Contract
The Path to Justice
You and Your Legal Rights
The Debt Collecting merry-Go-Round

Health
Guide to Combating Child Obesity
Asthma Begins at Home
Explaining Aspergers and Demenita

Explaining Parkinson's
Explaining Autism Spectrum Disorder
Children's Health-Combating obesity
Detox Naturally
Finding Asperger Syndrome in the Family-A Book of Answers
Reversing Osteoarthritis
Ultimate Nutrition Guides
Understanding depression
Guide for Cancer Sufferers and Their Families

Music
How to Survive and Succeed in the Music Industry

General
A Practical Guide to Obtaining probate
A Practical Guide to Residential Conveyancing
Writing The Perfect CV
Keeping Books and Accounts-A Small Business Guide
Business Start Up-A Guide for New Business
Writing Your Autobiography
Writing True Crime
Being a professional Writer

For details of the above titles published by Emerald go to:

www.emeraldpublishing.co.uk